"Candice Mummert's book is FANT[...] and humility, and based on the rea[...] a mother, Candice beautifully shar[...] subject of marriage. *From Single to [...]* traditional Christian values with 21st-century life in a compelling book that you won't want to put down. If you are a man or a woman considering marriage and want a GREAT marriage that honors God, this book is absolutely right for you."

—Brett Blair,
High Performance Life Coach,
author of *From Autopilot to Authentic*

"Hats off to Candice Mummert for her perspective on marriage in the 21st century! In *From Single to the Knot*, Candice takes the reader back to Scripture to discover the essential elements that make marriage work. This book is a solid reminder of this important spiritual union."

—Nancy Erickson,
The Book Professor,
author of *Stop Stalling and Start Writing*

From Single to

The Knot

How to Make the Knot
Worth Fighting For

CANDICE MUMMERT

LUCIDBOOKS

ISBN 10: 1-63296-161-X
ISBN 13: 978-1-63296-161-7
eISBN 10: 1-63296-162-8
eISBN 13: 978-1-63296-162-4

Table of Contents

*The words on these pages are dedicated to my children—
Ashlee, Abbie, Cailey, Nicholas, and Isaiah—as well as their future
spouses. May God guard and guide your hearts.*

Preface

Relationships are tough! Friendships can be either life-giving or life-sucking. Familial relationships can build us up or tear us down. Dating relationships can go from being something we practically beg for to being something we wish we could forget. And being single is not easy either! Singles face the waiting, the wondering, the questions, and the doubts about their future and their destiny. They also have to manage temptations, hopes, and dreams while they wait. It's complicated!

Then there's marriage, a relationship God intended to be lifelong and life-giving. Marriage was designed to be the ultimate partnership—one that makes us stronger by encouraging, supporting, and loving us while challenging us to love beyond our own feelings and abilities. Our society has a dishonored way of thinking about marriage. First of all, people feel pressure to find a spouse. Because so many aspects of society are designed for couples and families, there is unintended pressure to get married. We typically assume that getting married is one of those natural progressions in life, so if everyone around you is getting married, there is added pressure for you to do it too. Society and Hollywood also lead us to believe that marriage will bring an undeniable spark that will never go away and that our spouse will fulfill and complete us. Worse, we talk about divorce as if it is an acceptable next step to any marriage. When the spark dims or we are unfulfilled by our spouse, divorce is seen as the acceptable next step.

We have all seen examples of successful marriages and broken ones. Let's define what we mean by the word *successful*. One definition of a successful marriage is that it didn't end in divorce. But more than that, I believe a successful marriage is one that the couple fought for. They didn't settle for living as roommates or just staying together for the kids. They worked through their struggles, their differences, and their heartbreaks. They worked to always love each other more deeply. They learned to forgive over and over despite their differences and disappointments.

Although I have seen many broken marriages, I am blessed to come from a mother and father who have been married 43 years and to have in-laws who have been married 42 years, and they are both still counting. Maybe that has something to do with my view on marriage. In the same way, many people come from families with broken or unhappy marriages, and that seems like a "normal" part of life for them.

Wouldn't it be wonderful if the tide could turn to change the way our society perceives marriage? Through healthy conversations, realistic expectations, and one-on-one support, we could once again see more loving, lasting marriages with divorce being a rarity that only happens when absolutely necessary. To change the tide, crucial conversations should start before engagements and marriages; singles must have healthy, realistic conversations about marriage, setting themselves up for a greater chance of success.

As I worked on this book project, I often ended up at one of my favorite coffee spots. One day, a close friend joined me for lunch, offering me a break from the screen and keyboard. She is one of my greatest encouragers for what God is calling me to. After lunch, she headed back to her car, or so I thought. A few minutes later, I saw her walking in the opposite direction and holding hands with her husband of 24 years. They were both smiling from ear to ear. I texted her right away to let her know I had seen her walk by, and this was her response: "I met him for a midday kiss, and he offered to walk 'his girl' back to the van. Ahhhh, love that man!"

That's the way it should be! Not every day, because there will be trying days. But on the trying days, instead of couples fighting against each other, they can fight for another day like the one my friend was having.

My heart has been tender toward marriages for many years. My husband and I have hosted small groups in our home to discuss the topic of marriage. God has brought couples into our lives and enabled us to support and encourage them through relationship struggles and trials. We were able to believe for their marriage when they couldn't.

So, when God inspired me with the idea for this book, it reinforced my desire to pour into marriages. Even more, I saw the need for people to step into marriage with more realistic expectations. What a difference it can make if singles choose their spouses with more awareness of what they are getting into and set their minds to a lifelong commitment.

Here's to waiting for the right one and committing for a lifetime!

Introduction

Marriage can be the most amazing relationship we experience on earth. In fact, I believe it should be. We use familiar phrases to describe a healthy marriage: "You complete me" or "You make me want to be a better person" or "You bring out the best in me." Most of us have a long list of ideas about what a healthy marriage could or should be.

Then there is the ugly side of marriage. Sadly, we don't need a list for this; we know the unhealthy picture of marriage all too well. This side of marriage evokes memories of the times we had to work hard at something in our relationship that we thought should have come naturally, the nights we fell asleep barely liking the person we had chosen to do life with, and the days we dreaded walking through the door after work because we anticipated another evening of nagging and fighting.

So many times, my heart has been energized by stories of healthy marriages and broken by stories of loveless marriages. How wonderful it would be to hear more stories of couples that thrive well into the later years of marriage. I would consider it a pure blessing to be a part of cultivating more stories of thriving, healthy couples. I would love to change the perception, expectations, and outlook on marriage today.

I do not have a perfect marriage. Let's just go ahead and get that out there. Often, when I tell people I'm writing a book about marriage, they want to know how long I've been married. They want to know if I am a credible author. In all honesty, my credibility comes from imperfection. No marriage is going to be perfect, easy, or always meet your every expectation. There is no such thing. Did you hear that? No human being can be perfect or meet your every need. My husband, Aaron, is wonderful but not perfect, and he is not even "everything I dreamed" my husband would be. I assure you he would say the same about me! In the same breath, I can say I wouldn't give him up or give up on our marriage for anything. We have something far more important than perfection.

Aaron and I chose from the beginning to fight through the hard times. In the moments when I have been so mad that I didn't want him to touch me, I stood firm, knowing that forgiveness would come and his arms would comfort me again. In the times when he left the house in anger and didn't want to be anywhere near me, I remembered my husband's commitment to reconcile before the sun went down. Marriage is worth fighting for and must be fought for.

Lies

Unfortunately, too many couples who walk down the aisle these days are unprepared to fight. They are unprepared because they believe one of the lies in our culture; that is, if you choose the right person to marry, everything will fall into place and work out. Therefore, if problems arise, something must be wrong with the spouse you chose. From this misconception, the second lie arises, which is that divorce is a better, easier option than fighting for the marriage. It has become acceptable and unquestioned for a couple to give up on their marriage and to divorce.

I am not talking about times when divorce is the only answer— situations in which one of the individuals is in danger. I am talking about situations when, more often than not, couples simply give up. Times get tough, trust is broken, and ending the marriage appears to be easier than fighting for it.

We also tell ourselves lies while we are single: "I'm running out of time to find the right one." "I'm not as important or complete because I haven't started a family." "I need to focus more on finding a date and less on my friendships." These lies can lead to poor choices when it comes to lifelong decisions such as marriage.

Perhaps you know a couple who began their wedding day thinking that divorce was an option if things didn't turn out the way they expected. We hear these stories all the time. Just the other day, I heard a young woman on a reality show talk about her marriage of four months. She discussed some of the things she loved most about her marriage, but she ended by saying she didn't know if it would last forever. My heart broke as I listened. Four months into her marriage and she was already saying that it may or may not last, as if she had no power over the outcome.

Her words are typical of the lies our culture has come to believe; that is, if the marriage is meant to be, everything will fall into place. It will just happen. If not, then the marriage simply didn't work out, and the couple can move on.

We don't have to look far to see the consequences of "moving on" and the other lie that divorce is easier. In most cases, divorce is not easier. On the same reality show, another woman said she wished someone had told her what divorce was like before she let her marriage crumble. Looking back, she would have tried harder to make it work, but at the time divorce seemed easier.

The Truth

There is another option. We are not powerless, and we don't have to leave our marriages up to fate. We were never meant to walk into marriage thinking that divorce is an option if things don't go as expected.

The truth is that marriage is a gift from God. It was created and blessed by God. He gave us tools to equip us to purposefully stay married. Divorce, on the other hand, was invented by man because of hard hearts. In Matthew 19:8, Jesus said, *Moses permitted divorce only as a concession to your hard hearts, but it was not what God had originally intended.* It takes a soft heart to make marriage work. It takes active work.

Marriage was created to give us the ultimate relationship of love. God is love. The love we receive from God helps us actively love others, including our spouse. Marriage should be the deepest, most complete, earthly relationship we have.

Ecclesiastes 4:9 says that *two people are better off than one, for they can help each other succeed.* The language in Ecclesiastes suggests that a couple should be on the same team, headed toward the same goal, lifting each other up for success. Just think how intimate marriage would be if a couple knew they were looking out for each other's good! With that mindset, your spouse has the potential to be your best friend, biggest supporter, trusted sexual partner, and ultimate confidant.

Throughout this book, we will unfold God's truth about marriage. We will consider how to prepare for and wait for a spouse. We will look at sex according to biblical principles and learn how to have the ultimate sex life. We will peel back the layers of why God created marriage and what God intended it to look like. We will define what it means to be a godly spouse and consider how a godly person should treat his or her spouse. We will learn how to look for the life partner God intended for us, and it's probably not a surprise that finding the right person involves more than physical attraction and having a good time. We will also take a look at the waiting that comes with being single, and you will discover how you can make the most of that time and turn it into anticipation.

In this book, you may read some ideas and suggestions about marriage that you have heard before, but I hope that you also find new ideas and gain new perspective. Perhaps your reason for wanting to be married will be altered a little. Your view of what it means to be a godly husband or a godly wife may be cultivated. Hopefully, your feelings about waiting for sex, your spouse, and God's plan to unfold will be transformed. Maybe being single and waiting will take on new meaning that brings you peace and anticipation instead of dread.

My prayer is that this book will inspire a revolution of how we live in singleness and prepare for and walk into marriage. My hope is that you will feel empowered as you wait for God to bring you into the lifelong, fulfilling marriage you were meant to have. May you feel the untapped potential at your fingertips as this book presents ideas about how to maximize that potential.

So, join me! Let's dig in and start a fresh conversation on marriage!

Chapter 1

The Wait

⁶Do not be anxious about anything, but in everything by prayer and supplication with thanksgiving let your requests be made known to God. ⁷And the peace of God, which surpasses all understanding, will guard your hearts and your minds in Christ Jesus.

—Phil. 4:6–7 ESV

God's Plan Is Worth Waiting For

Chris Hodges, pastor at Church of the Highlands in Birmingham, Alabama, began a parenting course by saying, "I can't help you if you are going to leave God out."[1] I feel the same way about marriage. Marriage is hard, and if you intend to leave God out, I'm confident I can't help you. No human on earth can have a successful and satisfying marriage without the overflow of grace and love that God offers us every day. The scripture at the beginning of this chapter from Philippians says that it is through Christ Jesus that we get peace that surpasses understanding. We can't get it ourselves. We can't leave God out. Let's look at the concepts in Philippians 4:13 piece by piece and discuss how they apply to God's plan for marriage.

"Do Not Be Anxious"

The progression of life can be lonely and lead us to a desperate place. Typically, you graduate from high school and then college. Most of us fully expect to find that special someone in the singles-rich environment of college. But what happens when you haven't fallen in love by the time you graduate? For many singles, the pressures begin to mount when it seems as though everyone else has found that special someone. Why not you? In some cases, your next step may be to purchase a place of your own and move forward with your career. This is okay for a little while, but then your friends start to have babies, and you may feel behind the curve and lonely—the single life can be very lonely. If only you had someone to come home to, someone to talk with about your day. You start to think that almost anything sounds better than another year alone. You think the relationship wouldn't have to be wonderful—someone that you like most of the time would be better than nobody.

Maybe you are still in high school or college and already fear your life coming to this. You play the "what-if" game: "What if I turn out to be an old maid?" Maybe you are single again after being married and wonder if you will ever find that level of companionship again. You miss some or all the parts of having a spouse.

It is easy to sit in the place of anxious worry and desperation, especially when your loneliness is growing. It is natural to wonder if God has completely forgotten about you as you wait and wait and wait. You may even question if God really does have perfect timing.

Settling for a marriage based on your need for companionship or convenience may seem like the only way out of the loneliness. The truth is that there is another way. You can learn to tap into some of that peace that Philippians says only comes through Christ Jesus. It really can be better to be single and learn how to receive that peace through Christ than to settle for a marriage simply for companionship or convenience. The good news is that God IS trustworthy, He DOES see you. and He does have reasons. He is preparing good things for you if you are willing to wait for them and not settle for something less.

> [24] *"The Lord is my portion," says my soul,*
> *"therefore I will hope in him."*
> [25] *The Lord is good to those who wait for him,*
> *to the soul who seeks him.*
>
> —Lam. 3:24–25 ESV

"Let Your Requests Be Made Known to God"

First and foremost, let's get this out there: You are never alone. To learn how to tap into that peace of Christ, you must recognize that God is always with you. I know that talking to God is not the same as talking to a friend whose voice you can hear audibly. But when you do "hear" God's voice, it far surpasses anything a friend or loved one has to say. I also know there are times when we really need a hug or someone's physical presence. Believe me, I'm a hugger. If you can dig deep and lean on God, the rewards will far exceed your expectation.

The Bible tells us that God meets our every need. It's okay to tell Him what you feel and what you need. In reality, He already knows exactly what you need, but He wants to hear it from you. As you are asking, you must also submit to and trust His plan. If you allow Him to consume you, you will be filled. By allowing Him to be your everything, you will be strengthened and able to wait for His timing and in His hope. There is no greater joy than that of the Lord. No man or woman will ever make you more joyful than the Lord. And from that joy comes strength. In Nehemiah 8:10, we are told that the joy of the Lord is our strength. That is only one of many passages in the Bible, telling us that our strength comes directly from God. Throughout Psalms, the writers proclaim that the Lord is our strength, refuge, and stronghold.

A powerful cycle of submission and strength can be created between each of us and God.

We submit our lives to Him by trusting and waiting, and we are filled with peace and strengthened for the journey. This cycle does not come easily. Our flesh wants instant gratification. We want to be accepted and fit into the norm of society. However, it is very evident that some of the things we desire do not bring lasting happiness. We must strengthen ourselves enough to submit to God. Just when we think we are going to break, He catches us, and there in His arms, we find everlasting joy and peace. Suddenly that spouse we were dreaming of doesn't seem so essential after all.

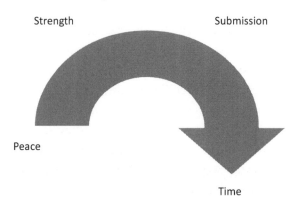

Strength   Submission

Peace

Time

I remember a time when I was waiting for the Lord's peace and had to submit and trust in my waiting. I had been deeply hurt by a very dear friend. Her words and actions had hit me in a way that made my chest burn with anger and disappointment every time I heard her name. Her actions stung more because she was a sister in faith. I expected more from her.

I first sought comfort and peace by talking it out with my husband and some close friends who were walking through the same thing. They had been affected by her actions and words in similar ways. I was comforted for the moment, but it didn't last. Inevitably, this person's name would come up in conversation, and my skin would crawl from my head to my toes. My chest would burn as it held in the pain and anger that wanted to come boiling out.

These physical triggers made me want to pick up my phone and call a girlfriend to release some of the pressure building inside and get the quick fix of peace. But I knew that peace wouldn't last even though my friend could relate to my anger and would validate my feelings.

I knew that it would only be temporary relief, and the situation did not need to be rehashed. On one occasion, after about 10 minutes of playing tug-of-war with myself, I prayed OUT LOUD right there in my car. I decided to submit my heart to what was true and let my requests be made known to God. I asked the Lord to start healing my heart and to guide me to forgiveness so that simply hearing her name wouldn't have so much power over my emotions. To be completely honest, even as I submitted to God, I was pretty convinced it wouldn't really work. At the very least, it might keep me from gossiping about my feelings, but I didn't think it would really make me feel better. And for sure, I didn't expect God to answer me audibly or change my heart. But do you know what happened? An amazing peace came over me right away. The burning in my chest subsided, I felt compassion for this friend, and my healing toward forgiveness started right then—not because of my perfect timing or perfect words, but simply because I submitted to God and turned to Him for my comfort. No friend or husband could have offered me that.

If you are in a position right now of waiting for a spouse, take a minute to recognize that you are not alone, ask for your heart's desire, submit and surrender to God's perfect timing, and be open to receiving the peace He has for you.

"By Prayer and Supplication with Thanksgiving"

While waiting, you can prepare for what you are expecting. The time can be spent growing into the person God is calling you to be. When you find a life partner, not only will you receive, but much will be expected of you as well. Use the wait to grow as an individual and prepare for who you will need to be as a spouse. There is someone on the other end of your dream waiting for you, too.

Don't waste today by not preparing for that person because you are too focused on tomorrow. To practice thankfulness when it is more natural to grumble and complain is a wonderful way to grow as an individual and prepare for who you will need to be as a spouse. Waiting is hard, and being thankful is the last thing we want to do when we are waiting. There will never be a time when you need to practice restraint about grumbling and complaining more than when you are married. You might as well start working on those thankful muscles now. As 1 Thessalonians 5:18–21 says, *Give thanks in all circumstances; for this is the will of God in Christ Jesus for you. Do not quench the Spirit. Do not despise prophecies, but test everything; hold fast what is good (ESV).*

Thank Him right where you are. No matter your circumstances, there is something you can be thankful for right now. I promise. Maybe you have many, many things to be thankful for, and you just need to remember them. Either way, being thankful for where you are and what you have will give you so much benefit. You will enjoy more, grow more, and love more. The Spirit is constantly guiding you. If you are unable to be thankful, the verses above seem to suggest that you will quench the Spirit. Think of all that you might miss. Be thankful and hold fast to what is good. Not only does this attitude keep our minds on right things, but it also keeps us from making a choice to grab for a spouse out of desperation and loneliness. It keeps us from making a decision out of fear.

"The Peace of God, Which Surpasses All Understanding, Will Guard Your Heart"

At the beginning of this chapter, we discussed the loneliness that can come from falling behind on society's unwritten timetable. Loneliness can lead to feelings of desperation that come from being left behind as we watch friends progress through stages of "growing up." Now, it's time to go a little deeper and recognize where that desperation has turned into fear. Peace and fear cannot coexist, and if it's true that peace guards our hearts, we need to learn how to make that switch.

The problem with fear is that it takes away our sound mind. In 2 Timothy 1:7, Paul says, *for God gave us a spirit not of fear but of power and love and self-control (ESV)*. Some versions use the words *power and love and sound mind*. Having a sound mind means we live in confidence that God has good things for us, and we can think clearly and positively about our future. That kind of thinking comes from God. Having fear means we live in insecurity and confusion. We fixate our minds on negative things and start to protect ourselves. That kind of thinking is not from God.

Mark Driscoll, a Christian pastor, called fear-based thinking "the false gospel."[2] More specifically, he said that fear preaches a false gospel. It seems to take over, and soon we are making our decisions based on fear instead of self-control and a sound mind. Fear-based thinking says that there must be something wrong with me if I'm not married yet. I am not a complete person, or I will never have a fulfilling life without that special someone. I'm running out of time—very soon, everyone good will be taken.

Driscoll went on to say that if your fear is being single, then your heaven is marriage, and your savior is your spouse. Is that powerful or what? Let's break that down a little bit. If you live in fear that you will be single for too long or forever, then your heaven is marriage.

Plain and simple, marriage is not heaven. I am blessed with a great marriage, but I still yearn for a place where all my tears will be wiped away—a place where there are no bad days. I yearn for a place where gut-wrenching heart work or huge sacrifices won't be needed on a regular basis. After all these years with my spouse, I have no doubt that heaven is light years better than marriage.

It follows that if your fear is being single, then your savior is your spouse. To unpack this, we first have to know what is meant by the word *savior*. The heart of the word is *save*. To live in fear of being single is to believe that your spouse will indeed be the one who will save you from loneliness, desperation, and a life of insecurity. Feel free to add your own ideas to my list; you know what you are hoping to be saved from. The problem with this kind of thinking is that you are putting something on your future spouse that he or she can't deliver. You are setting your future spouse up for failure, and you are setting yourself up for huge disappointment. No human being can come close to loving or sacrificing the way Jesus did. The failures experienced in marriage can bring an even deeper loneliness, desperation, and insecurity than being single. for this reason, even in a great marriage, Jesus must continually fill the couple before they can love one another the way they need to be loved.

In college, I had a dear friend who was in a committed relationship for much of our college years. When she talked about her boyfriend, more often than not, she would share how he wasn't what she was hoping for. He didn't seem emotionally invested, their priorities were different, and he was avoiding further commitment. She was really hoping that those things would work themselves out and that they would get married.

She said she felt that she had invested so much time in their relationship that she didn't want her investment to be for nothing. The idea of starting over made her feel old, like she would be running behind in the relationship race. She was not living with a sound mind or self-control. Her fear of being single or not being married by a certain age controlled her decisions.

Many people find themselves walking down the aisle simply because they're afraid of living life single. Some of this simply comes from peer pressure—or even family pressure. We're all expected to find a spouse, so we feel pressured to do so, even if that isn't God's plan for us. Single living is always better than settling for a marriage out of convenience, pressure, or fear.

What about you? Does my friend's story resonate with you? Has fear preached a false gospel to you? What are some of the fears you have about being single or being married? Have you been making

> *Have you been making decisions from a spirit of love, self-control, and a sound mind? Or have you been making decisions out of fear?*

decisions from a spirit of love, self-control, and a sound mind? Or have you been making decisions out of fear?

In the waiting time of singleness, we can obtain peace. We are not alone. God wants to know the longings of our hearts. He wants us to ask Him for the desires of our hearts and then submit to His timing. He wants us to grow our thankful muscles while we wait and recognize the areas in which we are controlled by fear. Using all these tools, it seems possible to apply the words of Isaiah 40:31: *But they who wait for the Lord shall renew their strength (ESV)*.

Without these tools, it seems impossible. We live in a world full of temptations. Our society is accustomed to instant gratification and very little accountability. Relational and sexual temptations are everywhere. How wonderful that God wants to renew our strength. He wants to guard our hearts with peace.

Once you have submitted your life to God's plan and chosen to trust Him, He is literally standing guard at the gates of your heart and mind. He is helping to protect you, and He puts up safeguards to preserve and prepare you for your future spouse. He will give you strength to say "no" when needed. How awesome is this image? We receive protection from the all-powerful God who offers us a strength and peace beyond our own understanding! Couldn't we all use a little bit more of that? As we press on through this book, we will uncover specific ways to make the most of what God offers us.

Shortly before I started working on this chapter, I was reading my devotional, *Jesus Calling*, and I found a beautiful message about waiting. I would like to share it with you.

> March 26
>
> Waiting on Me means directing your attention to Me in hopeful anticipation of what I will do. It entails trusting Me with every fiber of your being, instead of trying to figure things out yourself. Waiting on Me is the way I designed you to live: all day, every day. I created you to stay conscious of Me as you go about your daily duties.
>
> I have promised many blessings to those who wait on Me: renewed strength, living above one's circumstances, resurgence of hope, awareness of My continual Presence. Waiting on Me enables you to glorify Me by living in deep dependence on Me, ready to do My will. It also helps you to enjoy Me; in My Presence is fullness of Joy.[3]

No matter where you are in the progression of life, you must strive to lay down your worry. Become more self-aware of any fears that are holding you back from thriving, and equip yourself to choose trust and receive strength. You will receive strength to be single with hopeful anticipation that God wants to give you good things, knowing that your wait is part of His plan. He does, indeed, see you, and He will lead you every step of the way if you let Him.

> *You make known to me the path of life;*
> *in your presence there is fullness of joy;*
> *at your right hand are pleasures forevermore.*
> —Ps. 16:11 ESV

Chapter 2

What Is True Love?

¹ *If I speak in the tongues of men and of angels, but have not love, I am a noisy gong or a clanging cymbal.* ² *And if I have prophetic powers, and understand all mysteries and all knowledge, and if I have all faith, so as to remove mountains, but have not love, I am nothing.* ³ *If I give away all I have, and if I deliver up my body to be burned, but have not love, I gain nothing.* ⁴ *Love is patient and kind; love does not envy or boast; it is not arrogant* ⁵ *or rude. It does not insist on its own way; it is not irritable or resentful;* ⁶ *it does not rejoice at wrongdoing, but rejoices with the truth.* ⁷ *Love bears all things, believes all things, hopes all things, endures all things.* ⁸ *Love never ends. As for prophecies, they will pass away; as for tongues, they will cease; as for knowledge, it will pass away.* ¹³ *So now faith, hope, and love abide, these three; but the greatest of these is love.*

—1 Cor. 13:1–8, 13 ESV

True Commitment and Love Are Worth the Wait

This passage is one of the most well-known scriptures about love and probably one of the most common scriptures read at weddings. Yes, it was read at my wedding! If I were to break it down using simple words, I would say that the things that might seem to be most impressive to God are least impressive. Even things full of power that involve wild spiritual gifting and painful physical sacrifice mean nothing. Love is more strongly valued by God. From my experience, the things of highest personal value come at the highest personal cost. If you value being fit, for example, the cost is dedicating time and energy to exercise long term. If you value graduating with honors or at the top of your class, the cost is putting extra hours and focus into studying. If you value growth in your business, the cost is countless hours organizing, networking, and promoting. In all these examples, you must go above and beyond the normal effort to achieve your goal. So, if God ranks love above impressive spiritual power or painful physical sacrifice, it only makes sense that love would come at high personal cost. It will be something that we have to work for and put in extra effort to build and make last.

Let's look more closely at the layers of the excerpt from 1 Corinthians 13. There is a lot of depth in this passage. Verses 1-3 describe gifts that require God's power and God's favor. Speaking in tongues requires an anointing of the Holy Spirit given by God. Wisdom and understanding are also both gifts of the Holy Spirit. We read about the seemingly impossible feat of having faith to move a mountain, but can you imagine doing it? Can you imagine giving everything you have to the poor and then turning your body over to be burned? And yet after doing any of these things, full of power and impressiveness, God says that they are nothing compared to love. Love must be amazing!

Specifically, 1 Corinthians 13 describes love using words such as *kind, patient, protect, trust, persevere*, and *hope*. Love is not envy, bragging, pride, self-seeking, anger, and keeping a record of wrongs.

Love requires a depth of character and humility in our relationships; it requires interaction with people. To be patient requires long-suffering, which implies there is suffering in the relationship. To be kind means to be adaptable, which implies things are always changing in friendship. Envy is always an emotion of selfishness we have toward others. Love requires us to put another first. Hope is looking for things to get better and never settling for less than they can be. These are just a few of the ways that love is described in scripture, and none of these character traits or feelings come naturally because we want things to be easy. We can expect love to be work.

Kinds of Love

We aren't used to using the word *love* to refer to hard work or a choice. We throw around the word *love* often and assume that the word speaks for itself, but that's just not true. Turns out there are different kinds of love–love that we experience on different levels and in different kinds of relationships. The first way we experience love is *phileo* love or brotherly love. This is the love that comes from common interests and goals. You often see this love between friends and coworkers.

The second way we experience love is *storge* love, which is sometimes dutiful and unfeeling but also instinctual and strong from common experience. Most often this is the love that is found within a family. For example, there is a love between siblings that exists simply because they share the same upbringing, memories, and training. Even when siblings don't get along, storge love kicks in, and they defend each other if someone outside the family threatens one of them.

The third way we experience love is *eros* love, which is self-gratifying and most often used to describe sexual love. Infatuation or lust falls in the category of eros; when your love revolves around physical feelings, you are experiencing eros. There is very little depth to *eros*. It is all about good feelings which, inevitably, will not last. This type of love is most commonly used in our culture for romantic love. The problem is that when the good feelings go away, there is not enough emotional depth to help couples stay together; they have nothing to fight for.

Finally, there is *agape*, which is love that comes only from God. Any time the Bible says something about "God's love" or "the love of God," it refers to agape. Thus, this kind of love is mentioned over and over again in the Bible. Agape is not based on feeling, but choice—the same choices we see in the 1 Corinthians passage instructing us to be kind, patient, and long-suffering. It's the kind of love you need to love your spouse unconditionally. Even when our spouse doesn't deserve it, we choose to love our spouse just as God continually offers that same kindness and patience to us when we don't deserve it. The cross is the best example we have for love in a marriage because in God's choice, His agape, He gave us His one and only son: *For God so loved the world that he gave his one and only Son, that whoever believes in him shall not perish but have eternal life (John 3:16 NIV).* Agape love is the kind of love that will make a marriage last. It is real, true love.

We are all born with a desire to be loved. Our first instinct is to fill that desire with eros love. Once those feelings of eros go away, we are stuck in an empty relationship, worse off than before because now we are wondering if this is as good as it gets. We wonder if anything will ever satisfy that longing deep within. Maybe you have even found yourself in a situation where you couldn't keep your hands off your boyfriend or girlfriend, craving that eros energy of touching that keeps you coming back for more, but deep down, you know the relationship is empty. You're left with that same longing and desire to be loved.

Author and speaker, Beth Moore, gives words to the emotions of that longing in her study, *Entrusted.* She said:

> Somewhere deep inside of us lodges a longing to be earnestly searched for and found by somebody wonderful.

We may try to deny it, outrun it, or anesthetize it. We may keep it well covered, strong-armed, and adequately smothered, but sometimes in the quiet or sometimes in the crowd, this longing still has a way of bubbling to the surface. It's too embedded in our nature to outgrow. Even the psalmist David, the man after God's own heart, grappled and groaned with longing. *O Lord, all my longing is before you; my sighing not hidden from you (Psalm 38:9 ESV).*[4]

Sometimes that longing gets the best of us, and we settle for less than God intended for us. Over time, we are convinced that a tolerated relationship is good enough and waiting won't get us anything better.

The truth is, seeking and waiting for a person who is prepared to enter into a relationship built on agape love, full of commitment and perseverance, is absolutely worth the wait. There is something better than settling, and there is someone out there who longs for that same thing.

Since the world is continually and loudly influencing us about eros love, we are used to it. We know it. We may just need to spend more time educating ourselves on the goodness of true love, so we grow to crave that more. The models of commitment and selflessness within marriage have been diminished to the point that we don't understand how there can be both sacrifice and physical attraction. We ask the question, "If I am being kind, patient, and not rude as it says in 1 Corinthians, who is going to look out for me?" We wonder if there can be happiness with such selflessness.

Entering into a marriage centered on true love may seem hard; it may feel like the opposite of filling the longing within you. The results in the end, however, will be that someone chooses you, knows you and still wants to be with you, and loves you no matter what. That is true intimacy, true love. With true love, it may seem that you are setting yourself up for constant hurt. Loving your spouse is not always easy, but it should not hurt. Being hard to love and actually hurting are two different things. You may not feel like loving your spouse all the time, but that is different from the pain of emotional or physical abuse. Abuse is never a part of true love.

On the difficult days, you can expect to feel passion, comfort, longing, frustration, anger, and annoyance. All these are natural feelings that come with the 1 Corinthians-type, agape love. The Bible gives us this command in John 13:34: *Love one another, as I have loved you (NIV).* The Bible tells us eight times to love our neighbors as we love ourselves. In Mark, for example, we read the following command:

> *30And you must love the Lord your God with all your heart, all your soul, all your mind, and all your strength. 31The second is equally important: 'Love your neighbor as yourself.' No other commandment is greater than these.*
>
> —Mark 12:30–31

If God has to command that we love one another, that means we need to hear it and be reminded of it. Loving others does not come naturally.

We need to be reminded that there is a better, more beautiful way than eros love, which is temporary. Agape love is lasting because it is based on commitment and choice. When times get tough, we can stand on that commitment to love no matter what. When she has nagged you one too many times about picking up your dirty clothes, you can bear it. When he forgets to pick up the milk on the way home even though it was the last thing you said to him before hanging up the phone, you can choose to be kind. When he hurts your feelings down deep and it burns, you can make that hurt known and then forgive him. When she ignores the hard work you put in every day at the office in order to pay the bills, you don't have to boast. You can choose love, and you can fight through the difficult times. It's hard! The easy thing to do is give up, claim you have fallen out of love, and focus on what you think makes the grass greener on the other side of the fence.

But true love—the kind of love that couples celebrate on their 50th wedding anniversary surrounded by their children and grandchildren—is the love you must choose over and over again, so that you can fight for it. In the end, you receive true intimacy, and everyone wins. You, your spouse, your children, your community, and closest friends all reap the beautiful gifts that are produced because you chose to love.

There are entire lessons and Bible studies on how to love your spouse and how to fight for true love. I highly encourage you to take advantage of those studies with your spouse as you begin your marriage. In the appendix, I have included a list of resources to help you get started. For now, let's learn more about true love so that you can continue to replace any quick-fix thinking with long-term thinking.

In Jimmy Evans's marriage seminar, *Lifelong Love Affair,* he shared an acrostic using the word *PASSION.* In this poem, he describes seven actions used in the process of dating and falling in love. As you begin to grow roots in a relationship that lasts, these actions should be a part of it.

Pursue me every day

Ask me if I'm happy and let me tell the truth without having to pay a price

Say what you like about me a lot

Say please and thank you and use good manners

I need for you to study me and learn what I like and dislike

Only put God before me

Never turn your heart away[5]

According to Evans, these actions create passion in the beginning of a relationship and marriage, and they rekindle the flame long after the wedding day. I would like to take a deeper look at each one and share a personal story from my marriage about how they have made a difference in my relationship with my husband.

*P*ursue Me Every Day

Pursuing each other daily is not hard when you are interested in the relationship—especially at first. You want to talk on a regular basis. You consistently set aside time to see each other. You make special plans for when you are together. You put forth effort to contact and spend time with one another.

Oh, the days when my husband and I first started dating! I remember many times that Aaron showed up at my front door with a single rose. It was a sweet reminder that he was thinking about me and preparing to see me. He really was romantic in the beginning.

Then we got married. I never saw it coming, and I know it wasn't intentional on his part, but every romantic bone in his body disappeared. I am not exaggerating. After 13 years of marriage, I took a wise friend's advice and communicated to Aaron what I really wanted. Instead of hoping he would figure it out on his own, I politely starting to make specific requests in hopes of getting a little bit of the romance back.

One weekend, I had planned a date night, and I really wanted him to give me a rose as a romantic gesture to let me know he was thinking about our date and preparing for it. I imagined my parents arriving to keep the kids and, as we walked to the car or maybe as we buckled our seat belts, he would hand me a beautiful single rose to remind me that he loves me and is still pursuing me. That was my sweet little fantasy.

It didn't go like that. My parents arrived before me, and as I walked in the kitchen where everyone was busy getting ready for dinner, Aaron said in passing, "Oh yeah, your roses are on the table." Much to my surprise, right there in front of my parents and children, he gestured me toward a rose bush sitting on the kitchen table in a green plastic container. Not only did I not feel pursued, I was embarrassed that everyone heard his words and watched my reaction. I calmly said thank you and made my way out the door as quickly as I could without being too awkward.

He has never really lived that one down, but he tried that night, and he keeps on trying. He truly does strive to pursue me, and I choose to give him grace if it doesn't quite look the way I dreamed it in my mind's eye.

Ask Me If I'm Happy and Let Me Tell the Truth Without Having to Pay a Price

Communication—especially healthy communication—is crucial in a relationship. Healthy communication means being able to talk openly about our feelings with all defenses down and feeling heard. We can feel like we are paying a price when our spouse gets defensive or tries to fix our feelings.

A good tool in communication growth is to recognize when feelings are not justified and when there is a need to work through them. We also need to know when to apologize and when to forgive. When listening, you may need to recognize that you have unintentionally hurt your loved one and ask for forgiveness.

Living this one out can be tough and may take years to grow into. This could very easily be one of those struggles that rears its ugly face over and over again. I remember having conversations with my husband and feeling like we were just repeating ourselves, rehashing the same thing for three years but never getting to the core of the problem. We had to talk about what caused our defensive walls to go up, so we could recognize them and fight to keep them down.

Once those walls were up, nothing else could be heard and nothing productive could happen. We got to a point where we had permission to say, "I'm feeling defensive," and that would help us to step back, take a deep breath, and then continue listening. It was almost as if we would put on a new set of ears so we could listen in a different way.

Say What You Like About Me a Lot

It's impossible to say too many nice things. Make the effort to compliment your special someone even if it doesn't feel natural. You may feel like you are repeating yourself, but the receiver hears it fresh every time. Kind words go a long way. Encouraging words are a great way to make a wife feel loved and a husband feel respected. Look for ways to speak positive truths over your loved one. As Proverbs 18:21 says, *Death and life are in the power of the tongue, and those who love it will eat its fruits (ESV).*

Aaron is great with words of affirmation. It is his primary love language, and his words build me up as a mother and a wife. I have had to grow, not only in accepting his compliments, but also in speaking words of affirmation to him. I remember him thanking me for doing the dishes once, and all I could think was, "It's my job." Later I realized it felt good to be recognized for my everyday responsibilities, and I needed to work harder to recognize Aaron in the same way. The more you practice affirming words, the more natural this action becomes, and it has the power to set the tone of your whole household.

Say Please and Thank You and Use Good Manners

Unfortunately, we often treat the people we love most worst of all. Have you ever noticed that? We tend to take for granted those who are closest to us. Don't forget your manners when you are with that special someone. Being courteous is a way of showing respect and love.

We have five children that we are teaching to use manners. During the season of my life when I was blessed to teach music at a private Christian school, one of my favorite things was how the students would speak to the faculty and staff. For the most part, they had such good manners, always saying *please* and *thank you*. Many students would even say *thank you* as they left my classroom. It almost brings a tear to my eye as I reminisce about it now. It was so endearing, creating a special place in my heart for those students. I remember thinking that this was the way I hoped my children would speak to adults. I believe with manners comes privilege, and I want that for my children. It can work the same way in marriage. The more I thank Aaron for the ways he loves and supports me, the more he will want to do it. Marriage is one of the easiest places not to use manners, but that doesn't mean it is right. Manners make room for more love!

I Need You to Study Me and Learn What I Like and Dislike

We are constantly changing and growing as individuals so we are never done learning about one another. Take note of the things your special someone is most interested in. It is just as important to know the things he or she doesn't like. This information will help you to meet his or her needs and perhaps even exceed them. You can use this information to support and love your special person more completely. It's how romance begins and grows.

This one comes very naturally for me. When Aaron mentions something he likes, I tuck that note away to surprise him when I need a gift idea. My favorite example of this is when Aaron mentioned creating a prayer space in our closet after watching the movie *War Room*. I couldn't have been more excited to create that space for us. Later that week, Aaron came home from work and found I had cleared the clutter and clothes from a section of our closet and put up a cork board to hold our prayer lists and memorization scriptures. It feels great to know you've been heard when sharing a want or need.

Only Put God before Me

This one should be a deal breaker. If you are at a serious place in your relationship and are thinking about committing your life to one another, only God should come before that person. God must come first because that is where we draw the love from which we then share with one another. In 1 John 4:19, we are told that *We love because He first loved us (ESV)* No activity or person should be more important. Once God is first, your life partner should run a close second.

Aaron leads the race on this one in our marriage. He sets an amazing example of disciplined prayer and study time. I am always being stretched to do better because of the example he sets, and I couldn't be prouder to brag on him for it. I know that he is able to love me more completely because he puts God first in all areas of life.

Never Turn Your Heart Away

When times get tough, stick together. If your answer to hard times is that you always need space or to date other people, your heart is not headed in the right direction. Hard times should pull a couple together, not drive them apart. The issues you face when you are married only get more complicated. So, if dating issues send you in different directions, that is not a good sign. In young love, people often take a break to reevaluate their relationship. That is not what we are talking about here. This is about running from every little problem—turning away from one another during tough times, rather than drawing near to one another.

In our 14th year of marriage, I remember that Aaron and I had a rather heated discussion. I was trying not to get defensive but was approaching those walls anyway. He, in turn, became defensive as well, and all of a sudden, he had had enough. He threw down the papers he was holding and briskly walked out the front door. I continued cooking dinner and was comfortable with giving him some space, while at the same time I reevaluated my own feelings and actions. The important part was that I knew, through our years of growing, after we both had time to calm down and step back from the disagreement, we would come back together and figure out where we had gotten off track. Eventually, we would come back to common ground. How did I know? Because we both agreed that our marriage was worth fighting for, and we wouldn't let any issue come between us. We would work through it and come out stronger on the other side.

A final point about agape love: It grows and changes. On the day of your wedding, there should still be a fair amount of eros love. Hopefully, you will feel so in love that you can't imagine loving your new spouse any more than you do right then. The truth is, at that point, your ability for true love is still young, and there is so much room for growth. Isn't that exciting? After years of marriage, growing through challenges, possibly starting a family, loving one another through good times and bad, your love will grow. My husband and I have talked about how much we loved each other on our wedding day compared to now. After 15 years of marriage, two big moves, four children, and suffering the loss of one of those children, we love each other so much more completely and deeply.

Love that is true and lasting grows. That is good news. By continuing the actions shared earlier in this chapter, fighting for your marriage, and choosing to love when it's hard, you will also enjoy and celebrate how much more you will love your spouse years down the road.

Chapter 3

¹Yes, it is good to abstain from sexual relations.²
But because there is so much sexual immorality, each
man should have his own wife, and each woman
should have her own husband. ³The husband should
fulfill his wife's sexual needs, and the wife should
fulfill her husband's needs.

—1 Cor. 7:1–3

But you can't say that our bodies were made for
sexual immorality. They were made for the Lord,
and the Lord cares about our bodies.

—1 Cor. 6:13

Sex Is Worth the Wait

How did it feel to read these verses about sex? Did it make you feel restricted and bound? Or did you feel free and empowered? Our view of God's intentions for us can have a significant impact on our sexual decisions outside of marriage. Many people see the Bible as a rule book that helps us be better people. Some say, "I don't need religion to be a good person. I can do that on my own." But they don't understand the relationship with a God who wants good for them. They feel restricted by God's good intentions.

God gives us boundaries to protect us and keep us from harm. If we follow His commands, we are covered by His umbrella of protection. I once heard a podcast by Ravi Zacharias where he shared about God's commands and the protection they offer. He explained that if we step outside of the guidelines, or commands that God has given us, we are likely to experience things that prove why we needed the protection or His truths in the first place. The natural consequences of our actions will confirm the Word of God, and why we need His commands to protect ourselves.

The truth is, there are natural consequences of sex outside of marriage. Sex is a good thing. It is a gift from God. When sex is between a husband and a wife, it is a way to practice selfless, true love within the safety of your commitment. Sex outside of marriage creates baggage that may never go away. It diminishes the gift you have to offer your spouse. It complicates the present and the future and leaves you dissatisfied. Hear me out. There are many people out there who would claim good sex is always satisfying whether in the confines of marriage or not, and in the moment, there IS physical satisfaction—directly followed by emptiness.

Author Jimmy Evans says, "Sin feels good at first but hurts for a long time."[6] With most things that give us a quick pleasure fix, we grab them to feel good now, but we pay a price later. This is the case with most sin, right?

I have tried to help my children understand this concept early on because I want them to be trained to choose good things for themselves, even if it's the harder choice. It is common for my son, Isaiah, to sit at the dinner table, pick at his dinner, and talk more than he eats. He makes it clear he is not thrilled with my dinner menu. However, I also know that 30 minutes after dinner when everyone has left the table and Aaron and I are cleaning the kitchen and sharing about our day, Isaiah will still be sitting there picking at his dinner. He tries to be clever about why he can't choose the hard thing and eat his dinner. He makes up reasons to justify why it really is good that he doesn't eat his food. One night, he said, "Mommy my tummy hurts." Complete with downcast eyes and a pouty lip for dramatic effect. Turns out, mommies are smart. Mommies know everything (wink, wink). I knew he was trying to avoid finishing his dinner, so I calmly said, "Okay, buddy, I hope you feel better by breakfast."

As he was getting down from the table, I promptly called the other four children to announce dessert: "Kiddos, dessert time!" Isaiah, in midstride climbing down from his booster seat, froze, and quickly looked up at me. I met his gaze and with a sympathetic tilt of my head said, "Since your tummy hurt too badly to finish your dinner, it sure doesn't need any dessert. Head on upstairs to get your PJs on. I will be up in just a few minutes." Oh, I can hear you now through my mother's voice, "Give the sweet boy some dessert. Bless his heart." But I would much rather teach this lesson at four years old, than to have him learn it later in life when it really matters!

As I train my children to understand natural consequences, I help them see that choosing what's easy means not getting something even better down the road. It is worth it to withhold dessert from my four-year-old in hopes that it will cause him to choose the hard things now to get the better things later in life. I'd like to think that creating that discipline in him will affect his marriage and also make him a better husband someday.

No matter how well we were trained as children, we have all suffered the sting of natural consequences in our adult lives. For example, we have chosen the pleasure of gossip and suffered the consequence later when the situation turned and people talked about us. But what about sex before marriage? What are the consequences? There comes a time when you have to make the decision, a huge choice that you can never take back. In the heat of the moment, when passion is pulsing through every vein in your body, is not the time to make that decision.

No Take Backs

Sex before marriage, or any sexual experience, is something you can never take back. When you decide to save yourself for marriage, you are wrapping up a gift that God only offers you once. Once that gift is opened, it cannot be re-gifted. Have you ever heard it described as a rose? The beautiful rose represents your virginity. As you have physical or sexual encounters with people, you peal the petals off the rose. The once full, untouched rose is now a bud on a stem. With each sexual encounter, you are giving away a petal of your purity. The petals cannot be put back on the rose.

Baggage and Hurt

There is no regret quite like prematurely giving yourself sexually, having petals pulled off your rose, and being left with only a bud. When you have given yourself sexually and the relationship ends, you realize you have wasted one of the greatest gifts you could ever give your spouse. Instead of being a more complete person, you have forfeited a piece of yourself and won't get it back.

This reality has an even sadder image. Once you get married, instead of a beautiful rose, you hand him a bud. When you enter into a committed marriage, you will bring in all that hurt and regret with you. So many of my adult friends struggle with sexual intimacy in their marriage because of this. One of my friends was in her mid-30s before she realized the problems she and her husband were having in their marriage were because of previous sexual experiences.

It is good to be reminded that forgiveness and healing are possible. Whether you are single or married, you can make a choice to forgive yourself and your sexual partner and start anew. Today can be a new day to save yourself for your spouse and enter into a new beginning or to work on the healing needed to restore marital intimacy. I am so proud of my friend whom I mentioned earlier. After eight years of marriage and two beautiful children, she has been on a two-year healing process and refuses to give up. Praise God! She believes in Jesus's healing, and she believes in her marriage. She is a great example of what it means to fight for her marriage and not give up when things get hard.

Slave to Your Whims

> *Just because something is technically legal doesn't mean that it's spiritually appropriate. If I went around doing whatever I thought I could get by with, I'd be a slave to my whims.*
>
> —1 Cor. 6:12 MSG

A slave to your whims! Who wants that? Those who feel restricted by God's plan experience freedom to do whatever they want. But this verse suggests that doing whatever you want leads to slavery. You will become a slave to your desires, addictions, and relationships. You won't actually be free. The desires of your heart will be in charge.

Pornography is an example of such slavery; it is stealing our freedom and binding us at an alarming rate. Fifty-six percent of divorces are affected by one or both partners having a compulsive desire for pornography, and there is proof that continued viewing of pornography reduces your sex drive and affects sexual performance.[7]

Being a slave to your whims will not prepare you for a life of serving your spouse. Instead, you will be unable to see anything other than gratifying your own needs.

Hollywood Facade

Young singles often talk about the desire to "test drive" sex before there's a commitment. Society has created a Hollywood facade around sexual intimacy and fed us an unrealistic lie that sexual encounters, even first-time sexual encounters, are beautiful and logistically easy. The movie makers focus on the heated passion instead of the "work" of sex so that we are drawn to watch it. Then we are drawn to want it.

One of my favorite love scenes is from the movie *The Notebook*. Not because this movie is a picture of true, lasting love, but because it makes romance look so passionate and irresistible that I could watch it over and over again. The main character is engaged to one man, yet runs toward an old lover. They get caught in the rain in a canoe on the most romantic body of water I have ever seen. They run to the house through the rain, hand in hand, laughing and flirting, after hours of sexual tension building up. We will stop there with the details, but you know what it's like. In almost every Hollywood love scene, clothes slip off at just the right moment, lighting automatically resets to romantic mode, mood-setting music fills the room in surround sound, hair falls perfectly around the face, and muscles glow in the moonlight . . . amen, amen, amen. Oh dear, let's bring it back to reality!

It is extremely unrealistic for anyone to have an experience like this. Sexual encounters, more often than not, are far less perfect than the movies make them out to be. Clothes do not slip off at just the right moment. Lighting does not automatically turn itself to dim. Mood music only comes on if you connect to your Bluetooth speaker and choose your make-out song list. The Hollywood facade creates a false expectation that leads us to strive for that same passion in our own relationships and marriages. We assume that instant chemistry is the sexual goal, and you either have it or you don't. Thus, this generation feels the need to "test drive," fearing they will end up with a sexually flat marriage.

This is ridiculous. Great sex is the opposite of the movies. It has nothing to do with your sex style matching or your bodies fitting together well. Sex is something that can always change and be made better. Good sex almost always takes practice over time. In the previous chapter, we talked about how love is a choice, not a feeling. There are lots of opportunities to choose love during sex in a trusting relationship. You can talk about what you like or what you would like to try, and then serve each other to gratify those desires. You can talk about what you don't like or what makes you uncomfortable, and serve your spouse in those ways too.

Chemistry between two people is real, but it's not true that you need it for a satisfying sexual experience in marriage. Hardly anyone talks about how sex in marriage can get better over time. I have never heard that discussed. Usually marital sex gets bad press. There is an assumption that you need to enjoy sex outside of marriage because being with one person for the rest of your life is boring. In my late thirties, I can testify that doesn't have to be true. I can honestly say that as my husband and I have both grown in our lasting agape love for each other, our sex life has grown in pleasure as well. "Test driving" a sexual experience only creates more baggage that you will have to deal with later in marriage.

A scripture from *The Message* speaks about the realities of sex in plain language:

> *There's more to sex than mere skin on skin. Sex is as much spiritual mystery as physical fact. As written in Scripture, "The two become one." Since we want to become spiritually one with the Master, we must not pursue the kind of sex that avoids commitment and intimacy, leaving us more lonely than ever—the kind of sex that can never "become one." There is a sense in which sexual sins are different from all others. In sexual sin we violate the sacredness of our own bodies,*

these bodies that were made for God-given and God-modeled love, for "becoming one" with another. Or didn't you realize that your body is a sacred place, the place of the Holy Spirit? Don't you see that you can't live however you please, squandering what God paid such a high price for? The physical part of you is not some piece of property that belongs to the spiritual part of you. God owns the whole works. So let people see God in and through your body.

—1 Cor. 6:16–20 MSG

Setting boundaries for yourself means that you know God created you as a unique creation that cannot be replaced. You value choosing the hard thing now because you trust that there is something sweeter in the long run. You trust that He made you for more than one-night stands and short-lived empty relationships.

Bitter to Sweet

Jimmy Evans, Founder and CEO of Marriage Today, has encouraging words for those who want to choose the hard thing now to get the better thing in the end. He says, "Obedience has a bitter taste at first but it gets sweeter."[8] Have you ever experienced that? If you have hung around friends who drink, you know the scene. It looks really fun in the moment, but the day after is miserable. The sweetness comes later when they are all hung over and in trouble, but you feel fine and have a great day ahead because you chose not to overindulge. Maybe it was hard to forgive the pain that someone caused you, but the peace that followed made the effort worthwhile. It may have been hard to choose the right thing in the moment, but the reward that followed was so worth it.

Remember the story of the friend who I began to forgive by simply talking to God instead of gossiping with friends? That step marked the start of the forgiveness process; about a year later, the

Lord convicted me that I was still harboring anger, which was only hurting me. I had an opportunity to choose the hard thing in the moment so that I could receive the better thing down the road. I needed to dig deep within myself to find complete healing. I took my pastor's advice and wrote her a thank you note. That's right; I began thanking her for all the ways I could think of that she had blessed my life. This obedience was definitely bitter at first. I would much rather have reminded her of how deeply she hurt me and explained how I thought she could have handled the situation differently. But that wasn't what either of us needed. Let me tell you, it's hard to be mad when you are reminiscing about good times. My mind meandered through fun memories of girl time, Bible studies, and baby showers. I chuckled under my breath and enjoyed a tear or two. I finished the letter, mailed it, and as God often does, He worked the timing perfectly for the letter to arrive on a day when it would bless her in a special way. We are not best friends; in fact, life has led us to different states, and we seldom see each other, but God worked a great healing in my heart that day. When our paths do cross, I look forward to hugging her and chatting.

It's a Marathon

Marriage is said to be a marathon, not a sprint. The same goes for following God's instructions. He is not about quick satisfaction, but lasting joy and happiness. The discipline it takes to save yourself for marriage is hard now, but it does yield rewards, and it will be sweet in the end. We need patient endurance to do the will of God.

I like what Hebrews 10:35–36 has to say about the process of this endurance: *So do not throw away this confident trust in the Lord. Remember the great reward it brings you! Patient endurance is what you need now, so that you will continue to do God's will. Then you will receive all that he has promised.* Scripture commands us not to throw away the confident trust we have in God. We need patient endurance as we continue to do the will of God. Then we will receive all that He has promised us.

Decide right now that all the good God has planned for your marriage is worth way more than any sexual experience you could have now. Then hold on to the strength you have as a child of God. Help yourself by setting up boundaries.

Struggling to have discipline amid heated passion can be compared to walking by the edge of a cliff. If your foot were to slip, you wouldn't know if you were going to fall one way and land on the grass, or plummet off the side of the cliff. The smart action is to avoid walking too close to the cliff's edge—that way, if you slip, you will be safely caught by the grassy top of the cliff. So it goes with sexual temptations. You can set yourself up for success, or you can push yourself to the edge of the cliff and hope you can withstand those heated moments of passion.

We were all teenagers once, and maybe you still are. The temptations are great. No matter how much you love Jesus, your hormones are raging. I once heard a mom say, "They are both great kids! They go to church together and pray together." This was her way of defending her decision to let her daughter and her boyfriend be alone in a bedroom. I couldn't help but feel a burning discomfort as I listened to those words. Everyone needs boundaries! I needed boundaries as a teenager. I had every intention of saving myself for marriage and still ended up in very tempting situations. There is a certain point in temptation where no amount of Jesus will keep your clothes on. I beg you, protect yourself from those situations. Set yourself up for success. Otherwise, you will end up with long-term disappointment.

Another way to set yourself up for success is to surround yourself with people who believe the same things you do and will support you. Don't hang out with people who are going to pressure you or even offer you the opportunity to step outside the boundaries you have set for yourself. Remember you are worth it. You are worth the wait, worth the no, and worth the boundaries.

The reward is truly sweet. After the waiting, you will have a spouse to whom you can give your whole self. You will be free of images and expectations from other sexual experiences. You will be free to create a sexual relationship with your spouse that has no restrictions. You can love one another completely and find complete satisfaction in your sexual intimacy.

Sometimes the sweetness develops very quickly and other times it takes years, but it is always worth the wait. With all the temptations in our society now, how can you begin to find the strength to resist until your special someone comes along? Let's end by reminding ourselves that God offers to give us the strength to carry out His will.

> [12]*If you think you are standing strong, be careful not to fall.* [13]*The temptations in your life are no different from what others experience. And God is faithful. He will not allow the temptation to be more than you can stand. When you are tempted, he will show you a way out so that you can endure.*
>
> —1 Cor. 10:12–13

> *The Lord gives his people strength. The Lord blesses them with peace.*
>
> —Ps. 29:11

Chapter 4

The Creation of Marriage

Then the Lord God said, "It is not good for the man to be alone. I will make a helper who is just right for him."

—Gen. 2:18

God's Real Intention

We've talked about so many things already. We've discussed waiting with anticipation for your spouse, clarified that true love is a choice not a feeling, and revealed the reward of purity versus the quick fix damage of premarital sex. In this chapter, we will turn the clock way back and look at the beginning of marriage. We will see that God created marriage and that He created it for a reason and with certain intentions.

Before we dive in, it would be fun to reflect on your own thoughts about marriage. This could be the first time you have thought about the meaning of marriage, and maybe you don't have specific ideas. Or maybe you have spent lots of time forming opinions about the topic. Later in this book, we will reflect on how you answered the questions in this section to see if any of your answers have changed. Grab a pencil and write down your thoughts and answers to the following questions. No one is going to ask you to share your answers, so there isn't any reason you can't be completely honest with yourself and write the first thing that comes to mind.

1. Why do people get married?
2. Do I want to get married someday? Why or why not?
3. What are the easiest parts of marriage?
4. What are the most difficult parts of marriage?
5. If I get married, what do I expect to get out of it?

Marriage Was Created by God

Going back to the beginning, before even the very first marriage, God created man, Adam.

> *⁸Then the Lord God planted a garden in Eden in the east, and there he placed the man he had made. ⁹The Lord God made all sorts of trees grow*

up from the ground—trees that were beautiful and that produced delicious fruit. In the middle of the garden he placed the tree of life and the tree of the knowledge of good and evil. ¹⁰A river flowed from the land of Eden, watering the garden and then dividing into four branches.

—Gen. 2:8–10

What a beautiful image! A garden full of green, lush vegetation with a river gently flowing through the middle. According to Genesis 2:15, Adam was created to watch over the garden. His days were filled with tending to this landscape that he called home. There were wild animals all around, and they were obedient to him.

Then, to make the scene even more complete, God provided Adam with the perfect helper. After finding no suitable helper among the animals, He made a woman that Adam named Eve, and she was to help him with his work. She was to support his work and share in the benefits of the garden.

¹⁸Then the LORD God said, "It is not good for the man to be alone. I will make a helper who is just right for him." ¹⁹So the LORD God formed from the ground all the wild animals and all the birds of the sky. He brought them to the man to see what he would call them, and the man chose a name for each one. ²⁰He gave names to all the livestock, all the birds of the sky, and all the wild animals. But still there was no helper just right for him.

²¹So the LORD God caused the man to fall into a deep sleep. While the man slept, the LORD God took out one of the man's ribs and closed up the opening. ²²Then the LORD God made a woman from the rib, and he brought her to the man.

> *²³ "At last!" the man exclaimed. "This one is bone from my bone, and flesh from my flesh! She will be called 'woman,' because she was taken from 'man.'" ²⁴ This explains why a man leaves his father and mother and is joined to his wife, and the two are united into one.*
>
> —Gen. 2:18–24

You may have heard someone say, "She completes me." Go ahead, roll your eyes. As cliché as it sounds, that is exactly what God had in mind, to complete Adam. Eve was the helper that was right for him. She would complete him, balance out his strengths and weaknesses, make him better. Your life journey should be made easier and more fulfilling with a spouse.

The scriptures use even deeper language than the word *complete*. The Bible says that the man and woman are united into one. This is a great mystery, and no doubt Adam was excited about it as he says, "At last!"

There was such innocence and purity in the beginning that Adam and Eve didn't even need clothes. There was no judgment, shame, or embarrassment—just beautiful days to enjoy God's perfect creation. Wow!

We could linger here and try to imagine married life as it was originally intended, but instead, let's look forward and see how the author of the Song of Solomon puts words to the enjoyment of his spouse.

> *¹ You are beautiful, my darling,*
>   *beautiful beyond words.*
> *Your eyes are like doves*
>   *behind your veil.*
> *Your hair falls in waves,*
>   *like a flock of goats winding down the slopes of Gilead.*
> *² Your teeth are as white as sheep,*
>   *recently shorn and freshly washed.*

Your smile is flawless,
each tooth matched with its twin.
—Song of Sol. 4:1–2

You have captured my heart,
my treasure, my bride.
You hold it hostage with one glance of your eyes.
—Song of Sol. 4:9

Delight exudes from this author—words that show emotional connection with depth. He talks about her physical beauty along with the fact that his bride has his heart.

Marriage still offers that same intimacy and depth today. It is a relationship that stands apart from any other human relationship we will experience. The relationship is emotional as we see in the Song of Solomon, it is rational in the ways that we use our thoughts to help and work together, and it is physical and spiritual as we mysteriously become one. No other relationship is this complete.

When marriage is done well, your spouse is the person you miss the most, your best friend, and lover. He or she is the one you want by your side to celebrate with, tell everything to, and hold your hand through dark times.

Why Did God Create Marriage?

In Ecclesiastes, we read that two are better than one.

⁹Two people are better off than one, for they can help each other succeed. ¹⁰If one person falls, the other can reach out and help. But someone who falls alone is in real trouble. ¹¹Likewise, two people lying close together can keep each other warm. But how can one be warm alone? ¹²A person standing alone can be attacked and defeated, but two can stand back-to-back and conquer. Three are even better, for a triple-braided cord is not easily broken.
—Eccles. 4:9–12

Marriage was created to give us strength

Ecclesiastes presents a convincing case for the benefits of having a partner. The examples are easily relatable. We can probably remember a time when we have needed help. We have all felt cold and either wanted the warmth of another or benefitted from having the warmth of another. We could stop there, but these examples were meant to be developed even more deeply. *Falling* could mean being emotionally heavy, sinking into sin, or not succeeding at a goal you have set. *Keeping warm* could refer to physical warmth, but it could also signify emotional warmth. God never intended for us to live life alone. We learn that from Genesis 2:18–24; God created Eve because He saw that it wasn't good for Adam to be alone. He is a God of relationship, and marriage is a gift of intimate, earthly relationship that He created for us.

Let's take a moment and look more closely at the very last part of Ecclesiastes 4:12. Instead of talking about two, the author (some think to be Solomon) talks about the strength of three. He refers to a triple-braided cord and how difficult it is to break. If you have ever tied off a boat with a triple-braided cord, you know about this strength. If you end up with your finger in just the wrong place, you wonder if you will get that finger back!

Usually when we think of a group of three, we don't think of strength. Three is a crowd, right? If the third party is a best friend that you are always confiding in or worse, a confidant of the opposite sex, then three IS a crowd! Those relationships can draw you away from your spouse and keep you from being on the same team. Those relationships are not the third party of strength in Ecclesiastes.

God is the third party, the third strand that strengthens marriage. He wants to be invited in, as an essential part of the covenant to make it stronger. By making God the center of your marriage, you will be strengthened and will be able to overcome the trials of life together, the strong triple-braided chord.

Aaron and I decided right away in planning our wedding that we wanted our first act as husband and wife to be taking communion.

Now, before you give us too much credit, it certainly wasn't a decision we made out of our Christian maturity. I just know that we desired for God to be the third strand in our marriage, so we started right there on the altar at our wedding. Taking communion means more to us now, and I am glad we did it at our beginning, even though our understanding of it was young. It is something I wouldn't change for the world. I know without a shadow of a doubt communion was the first step for us to make God the third party in our marriage, and there have been times when God has carried us side by side because we didn't want to walk side by side, if you know what I mean. Thank you, Jesus, for your strength in our weakness.

Marriage was meant to be a haven for individuals to grow and succeed

Another verse that helps us to understand God's purpose in creating the marriage covenant is 1 John 4:12: *No one has ever seen God; if we love one another, God lives in us, and his love is perfected in us (NRSV).* Thus, another benefit of having God as the third strand is his active partnership in perfecting us in our love. Our number one order from God is to be in relationship with Him and to love one another. Love God, and love people. It's all about love. In healthy marriages, individuals grow in many ways. One of the most profound areas of growth is love as marriages are tested time and time again.

Many times, selfishness rears its ugly head or forgetfulness leads to an important dropped ball. Consider these examples and ask yourself how you would respond if:

- Your husband did nothing for your anniversary—again.
- Your wife turned you down in bed for the fifth night in a row.
- Miscommunication got the best of you. Your husband claimed he didn't hear your plans for a busy weekend even though you remember telling him, and he blames his miserable weekend on you.

- You haven't even taken your shoes off after getting home from work, and she is already nagging you about changing the light bulbs that burned out.
- You lost your job and feel like you are losing your identity.
- You lost a child and now feel like you are losing one another.

How did it feel to read through these scenarios? Was your natural response patience and understanding? Or did you feel stress just thinking about these scenarios? Sometimes in the moments of stretching, real agape love seems impossible, and if God weren't living inside you, it would be impossible. In those moments, it may feel like growth is not happening, but God's plan is to perfect you over time. You won't see the growth all at once. But over the years, you will be able to look back and realize that you have found new ways to communicate. You have gotten better at deep breathing and exercising patience. You have learned to compromise in big ways and in small ways. Over time, it becomes easier to put your spouse's needs first. Just like the ring on your finger, you will create a beautiful circle of love and forgiveness.

Marriage should be a training ground for how to love more completely. Sometimes, it will look messy or even downright ugly, but that is all part of the growing process. God can use the marriage relationship to mold us into the people He created us to be.

Marriage was created as a base on which communities are to be built

From 1 John 4:12, we can see that if we love our spouse, God's love is perfected in us. That same dynamic of love applies if we are loving those in our community as well. As you grow in your ability to love at home, you will also grow in your love for others outside the home. As you receive God's perfect love, it is nurtured by and shared with your spouse and will automatically flow into your community.

Many people will come into your life over the years. Some will be easy to love and others very difficult. All the same, God calls you to love them. You might love a friend through a difficult time, stand strong with a coworker who needs to lean on you, or serve in your church. As your ability to love grows, your friendships will grow and will have a domino effect on those around you. People will be attracted to join your circle of friends, and community will be created.

Just as a healthy marriage leads to a healthy family, a healthy family leads to a healthier community. Marriage offers a safe place to practice showing love, so that you can better love other people God brings into your life. As you grow in your marriage, you will no doubt influence and bring change to individuals and your community.

God's Intention for Marriage

A man leaves his father and mother and is joined to
his wife, and the two are united into one.

—Matthew 19:5

Marriage was intended for commitment

In a friendship, when things go bad, you can walk away. If a friendship doesn't work out, two people go their separate ways. There are seasons for friendships, and many of them are not meant to last a lifetime. However, marriage is meant to last a lifetime. In marriage, we have the great mystery of two becoming one. How do you separate one person? How does one person go his or her separate way?

If it is true that God sees you as one, walking down the aisle is something to take seriously as a binding commitment. Because of this, marriage begins with an oath between one man and one woman taken before God; they promise to love and cherish one another until death parts them. Consider the following example of a traditional wedding vow. It sums up what God intended quite nicely.

> I, (name), take you, (name), to be my [opt: lawfully wedded] (husband/wife), my constant friend, my **faithful partner** and **my love from this day forward**. In the presence of God, our family, and friends, I offer you **my solemn vow** to be your faithful partner **in sickness and in health**, in good times and in bad, and **in joy as well as in sorrow**. I promise **to love you unconditionally**, to **support you in your goals,** to **honor and respect you,** to laugh with you and cry with you, and to **cherish you** for **as long as we both shall live.**

Wedding vows mean more with every passing year of marriage. Each phrase of the vow has an experience to go with it—times of joy and sorrow, sickness and health. On our wedding day, Aaron and I could never have imagined how much our love would grow with each year and each life experience we would share. We fully loved each other on our wedding day, but our capacity to love over the last 15 years of doing life together has increased greatly. Through good times and bad, arguments and laughter, we have grown to know each other so much more completely. If we ever renew our vows, we both believe it would be a very different experience the second time around. Our memories would give our words so much more depth.

There is something beautiful about a couple walking down the aisle with a desire to fully commit to the relationship, knowing they are about to become one. There is also a beauty in what that commitment creates. Commitment creates a framework of safety and trust for a lasting, loving relationship. Without commitment, there is always an underlying question, "Will I do something to make her leave?" If this is the question, you will be insecure every day about your actions, and you will do things to make her want to stay. However, if you both decide to fully commit, you will have the assurance of knowing that your spouse will stay when times get tough. You are free to be yourself, to be known and loved no matter what. As you work through things, you and your spouse grow and become better individuals. And as you learn to compromise and forgive, you become a stronger couple.

Marriage was intended to be honored

We all know couples who value commitment but are miserable because they stay together yet ignore the rest of their vows to forgive, support, or even stay faithful. Such couples experience no growth in love. God doesn't just want us to commit to staying together; he wants us to honor marriage and receive the joy of our commitment—the whole package.

Hebrews 13:4 says, *Give honor to marriage, and remain faithful to one another in marriage.* The commitment of marriage is not to be taken lightly. It is a vow taken before God. The meaning of those vows should be taken seriously and carried out; marriage is a gift from God. It is to be honored above all other human relationships and prioritized as such.

One of the lines usually recited during a marriage ceremony is, "What God joins together, let no one separate." Not only does this statement remind us that God is an essential part of the union, but it also shows that marriage should be held in such high esteem that *nothing* is allowed to overcome it. So, what does it mean to honor a relationship? In the *Merriam-Webster Dictionary*, the following words are used to define *honor:*

- Public esteem
- Merited respect
- Superior standing
- Symbol of distinction
- Chastity (purity in conduct and intention)

- Purity
- Integrity

There is serious strength in that list of words. To be honored is a symbol of distinction; that means marriage stands out from other relationships. To have integrity also means to be incorruptible. Bringing chastity into the definition means we honor our commitment, not only with our actions, but also with our intentions. By honoring marriage, you hold it in high esteem, allowing it to stand out from all other relationships and guarding it against corruption. Isn't that what we should do with such a precious gift that God has given us?

Submit to One Another

Commitment is the backbone, but honor gives importance to vows and the relationship, and submitting to one another gives a clear and precise picture of what God expects of the wife and husband. In Ephesians, Paul offers encouragement for living according to God's law. Within these instructions Paul explains the mindset we should have as we live and carry out our vows.

> [21] *And further, submit to one another out of reverence for Christ.*
>
> [22] *For wives, this means submit to your husbands as to the Lord.* [23] *For a husband is the head of his wife as Christ is the head of the church. He is the Savior of his body, the church.* [24] *As the church submits to Christ, so you wives should submit to your husbands in everything.*
>
> [25] *For husbands, this means love your wives, just as Christ loved the church. He gave up his life for her* [26] *to make her holy and clean, washed by the cleansing of God's word.* [27] *He did this to present her to himself as a glorious church without a spot or wrinkle or any other blemish. Instead,*

she will be holy and without fault. ²⁸In the same way, husbands ought to love their wives as they love their own bodies. For a man who loves his wife actually shows love for himself. ²⁹No one hates his own body but feeds and cares for it, just as Christ cares for the church. ³⁰And we are members of his body.

³¹As the Scriptures say, "A man leaves his father and mother and is joined to his wife, and the two are united into one." ³²This is a great mystery, but it is an illustration of the way Christ and the church are one. ³³So again I say, each man must love his wife as he loves himself, and the wife must respect her husband.

—Eph. 5:21–33

Wives are to submit to their husbands, and husbands are to love their wives. There is much more to that command than meets the eye. Paul compares the husband's love to the death of Christ. The husband is the servant leader of the home, and he lays down his life for his wife. The wife then submits to his servant leadership and shows respect. Again, this is simplifying this passage to its most basic picture. However, even in its simplest form, this scripture illustrates the beautiful cycle that is created when a husband lays down his life for his wife as she needs to be loved and a wife respects her husband the way he needs to be respected. This is such an important part of marriage that there are complete books written on this one topic and how to successfully do it. The expectations for both husband and wife are connected back to the relationship between Christ and the church.

Husbands

Christ is the head of the church as the husband is to be the head of the home. Christ loves the church unconditionally, enough to give His life for it. Thus, husbands must find the most complete, selfless way to love their wives. As my husband continued to step up to the challenge of loving me the way I was asking to be shown love, he did so in a way that he knew I would appreciate, and, in one instance, it ended up being quite humorous.

The year our oldest turned nine, my husband treated me to a wonderful Mother's Day. Gifts and quality time didn't rank very high in his love languages, so my previous eight Mother's Days were breezed over without much thought. So, on this Mother's Day, I was lovingly overwhelmed by breakfast in bed, homemade cards from all my children, lunch out, and then a movie with some of my girlfriends.

It was a magnificent day, and as I rode home from the movie, my heart was full to the brim! As my friend dropped me off, I was smiling from ear to ear and looked forward to thanking my husband for such a wonderful day. It was late, so the family was asleep, and the house was dark. I entered the password onto the keypad to let myself into the garage. Then I proceeded to take my shoes off and open the door between the garage and the house. It wouldn't open. My husband had locked me out!

Bless him, he had gotten the children to bed and then continued with his nightly routine to check the doors and set the alarm. I didn't have any keys with me because I didn't drive to the movie, and we didn't, and still don't, have a hide-a-key. Not only that, if I had been able to get myself in I would have set off the alarm and awakened everyone in the house in one of the most startling ways possible.

I began texting my husband's phone, hoping to gently awaken him so he would come let me in. When that didn't work I called his phone. That didn't work either, so I began to knock on the door. No response. I proceeded to the front door and knocked there. Still nothing. By this time, at least 20 minutes had passed, and I needed to use the restroom. My soda at the movies had worked its way into what was now a very full bladder.

It was time to get strategic. I began spacing my texts and calls, trying to create a pattern that might wake my husband. I never dreamed I would be strategizing in this way, but my bladder was desperate and I didn't want to pee in the back yard! It was no use. So, 45 minutes into this ordeal, Aaron and our children were still sound asleep.

Clearly, I had to submit to being outside, but still, I was not quite ready to submit to a fate of relieving myself next to my children's swing set. I made myself a pallet on the garage floor with a couple of sleeping bags. After another 15 minutes of my bladder screaming at me and no comfortable position to be found, I decided to add the doorbell to my strategy. I was no longer trying not to wake the children. I was desperate to wake anyone! Devising a rhythmic combination of texts, calls, knocks, and bell rings, I began a dance between the front door and the garage door. Finally, help came.

An hour and a half after my friend dropped me off, my husband timidly opened the garage door and peeked out with a half grin on his face. Before he could say anything, I pushed past him to the bathroom. Honestly, I don't remember what was said that night, but I do remember we were both laughing about it the next morning. The story is a good illustration of how my husband intentionally tries to love me, even when it doesn't end up all roses and chocolate.

Wives

As Jesus was willing to lay down his life for the church, in turn, wives should strive to respect their husbands. As the church looks to Christ for leadership, so wives should look to their husbands for direction, always showing them respect. I see ways that I have done this well, and not so well.

In the days when we had three daughters between the ages of newborn and five years old, there was one year when I had all three of them home with me. I could hardly wait for four o'clock to roll around so that Aaron would be home from work and give me a little breather. There were days when I couldn't hand them off fast enough to finally get a shower that was long overdue!

However, I had to really dig deep to honor and respect the fact that he too had worked all day and had been pulled in many directions. I was by no means good at this in the beginning, but I learned to honor the work he was doing for our family by giving him time to decompress from his day. If I respected him in this way, he could feel ready to step into the role of daddy, and the rest of the evening always flowed better!

> Honey, I'm sorry for the many days I forgot this step and threw children at you before you could get your coat off and without saying hello. Oh, and for the days I purposefully put off changing the poopy diaper or feeding them a snack because I knew you would be home soon, and I could hand them off just in time. Love ya' lots!

Ephesians 5:21–33 begins with, *submit to one another out of reverence for Christ.* Having Christ as the center of our submission is very important. Without Christ, submission can feel heavy or one-sided. With Christ, there is a mutual serving for the other's good. Submission with Christ as the center is based on sacrifice and mercy. We aren't always loving or respecting one another because our spouse deserves it or because we feel like it. There are days when we must choose these actions, beyond our feelings, out of devotion or admiration for Christ.

Let's go back and reflect on the questions you answered at the beginning of this chapter. Did any of your answers include the ideas discussed in this chapter? Would you answer any of those questions differently now?

Marriage is a framework within which you can grow. Commitment provides the security and safety to be yourself and practice mercy toward one another. It should be the safest relationship you have. It is a training ground for loving others and influencing your community. Marriage is an opportunity to honor God and His purpose for marriage as well as honoring your spouse.

Chapter 5

What Are the Roles of Husband and Wife?

*Give honor to marriage, and remain faithful to one
another in marriage.*

—Heb. 13:4

*J*n the last chapter, we discussed who created marriage, why it was created, and its intended purpose. This chapter looks at the role of the husband and the role of the wife. It will be helpful to know what is expected of you and what you can expect from a spouse, so you can encourage your spouse in his or her efforts.

It is essential to remind ourselves that God created the partnership between the man and woman for good. Remember from Genesis that, after God created all the animals, Adam still wasn't satisfied; there was no suitable partner for him. Genesis 2:20 tells us that *He [Adam] gave names to all the livestock, all the birds of the sky, and all the wild animals. But still **there was no helper just right for him** (emphasis added).*

God's response to Adam's lack was to put him to sleep and take one of his ribs. Therefore, Adam and Eve were literally made from one flesh.

> *[21]So the Lord God caused the man to fall into a deep sleep. While the man slept, the Lord God took out one of the man's ribs and closed up the opening. [22]Then **the Lord God made a woman** from the rib, and he brought her to the man.*
>
> *[23]**"At last!" the man exclaimed.** "This one is bone from my bone and flesh from my flesh! She will be called 'woman' because she was taken from 'man.'"*
>
> —Gen. 2:21–23; emphasis added

It is significant that God made the partner for Adam out of his own body. In a Bible commentary by Jamieson, Fausset, and Brown, I read a beautiful explanation of how and why God created woman: "She was not made out of his head to surpass him, nor from his feet to be trampled on, but from his side to be equal to him and near his heart to be dear to him."[9]

Throughout the rest of this chapter, we will look at what God expects from a wife and a husband. In Genesis 2:21–23, we are given a beautiful image of two people created to be partners. God first gave Adam the animals, and he had dominion over them. Then God gave Adam the perfect partner in Eve, and one was not made to stand over the other. Adam did not have dominion over Eve. I love how the quote from the commentary says they were created to stand side by side as equals, very special to one another, and above all other human relationships.

Let's be honest. All over the world, we see marriages that are not designed to be equal partnerships. In some cases, the marriage system benefits the man, or he doesn't have to hold his wife dear. In other instances, women are forced to get married to further the family lineage; wives are deprived of all personal rights; men take more than one wife; wives are to be seen and not heard, and they must walk one step behind the husband, head lowered and eyes toward the ground. In America, women have more freedom, but we still see a lack of the partnership of marriage from both the men and women. Husbands are tempted to control their wives, and wives are tempted to degrade and nag their husbands. God created marriage to be so much more.

Unfortunately, we tend to live out the examples set before us. If God's model of partnership isn't what we saw growing up, we tend to conduct our marriage according to what we witnessed from our parents, relatives, movies, and others around us. We bring expectations into marriage according to the marriages we witnessed growing up—whether good or bad. You may not even realize how much you've been influenced and how the behaviors you saw growing up have been imprinted on you as normal. You have internalized actions and values that you expect to apply in your own marriage. Some of these are good expectations, but some will bring distress to your marriage. Some will be small matters that are easy to resolve if you take the time to recognize them, but others will be very difficult to resolve because they are so deeply rooted.

Here are a few examples:

- The husband should always double check the doors and secure the house before bed because that's what my father did.
- The wife should make the bed every morning because that's what my mother did.
- It is better to stay quiet about little things that bother me than to bring them up for discussion.
- The husband pays the bills and takes care of the budget, and the wife need not be involved.
- Sex happens whenever and however the husband wants it.

Learning to be equal partners in marriage takes time because the way we were raised created values that may conflict with the values your spouse brings into the marriage. Also, men and women were created with different needs, desires, and responsibilities. They were created to love and be loved in different ways. The Bible gives us very specific directions on this. That doesn't make it easy, but it does give us guidelines to help us succeed.

HUSBANDS

What does it mean to be a husband according to God's plan? The creation story gives us the foundation of husband and wife working together as equals, not one above the other. How can the husband partner with and honor his wife?

The first step in partnering with a wife is to receive her as a blessing. We remember that when God created Eve, Adam's response was, "At last!" The author of Proverbs gives us more insight for the husband on this matter. Let's read the verse in two different translations:

> *He who finds a wife finds a good thing,*
> *and obtains favor from the Lord.*
>
> —Prov. 18:22 ESV

Find a good spouse, you find a good life—
and even more: the favor of God!

—Prov. 18:22 MSG

According to this verse, having a wife is a good thing. *The Message* says that a wife will give you a good life! Beyond those two things, there is favor. Have you ever thought that having a wife would bring you favor? To have favor is to be accepted and receive grace. God is happy to give you the relationship with your wife. God sees marriage as a blessing: a wife is good; your life will be good. Ecclesiastes 9:9 gives us an even more specific word for God's blessing and says that the wife is the husband's reward: *Live happily with the woman you love through all the meaningless days of life that God has given you under the sun. The wife God gives you is your reward for all your earthly toil.*

In Ecclesiastes, Solomon writes about the meaningless days of life. This life is not the endgame. There is so much more that awaits us in heaven, and compared to heaven, our time on earth is insignificant. Yet God blesses us during our time on earth with rewards. Specifically, the man receives a reward in receiving a wife. A reward is the product of a job well done, and a reward is usually something we look forward to. She is a reward for "earthly toil" or work on earth. It matters that God gives a wife in reward for the husband's work. When something is a reward, you take care of it and cherish it.

As you prepare for marriage, it makes sense that you would seek fulfilling work as well as prepare to receive the reward:

- Seek to understand your God-given gifts and what makes you thrive.
- Find confidence in being a child of God.
- Learn to accept mercy, forgiveness, and love from God. Then practice giving mercy, forgiveness, and love to others, so you will be able to give them to your wife.

- Pursue education, work, career preparation, and financial stability.

Give your future wife the gift of being prepared. Your earthly work will pay off as you begin to share the life you have created with the wife God brings you.

A husband puts his wife's needs before his own

A wife is good, dear to the husband, and a reward. Now, how does God describe the daily life of a husband? What are his responsibilities? We've already laid the foundation for this in chapter 4, using Ephesians 5:21–31. The husband's role is to lay his life down for his wife, just as Christ died for the church. This is the larger picture of the husband's role beyond the stereotypes of who does the dishes or mows the lawn. The responsibilities we are referring to in this chapter will get more specific and relate to the bigger picture. These attributes of the larger picture lay the groundwork for a healthy, flourishing marriage that can survive the test of time. Let's read the Ephesians passage again.

> *[21]And further, submit to one another out of reverence for Christ.*
>
> *[22]For wives, this means submit to your husbands as to the Lord. [23]For a husband is the head of his wife as Christ is the head of the church. He is the Savior of his body, the church. [24]As the church submits to Christ, so you wives should submit to your husbands in everything.*
>
> *[25]**For husbands**, this means love your wives, just as Christ loved the church. He gave up his life for her [26]to make her holy and clean, washed by the cleansing of God's word. [27]He did this to present her to himself*

as a glorious church without a spot or wrinkle or any other blemish. Instead, she will be holy and without fault. [28]In the same way, husbands ought to love their wives as they love their own bodies. For a man who loves his wife actually shows love for himself. [29]No one hates his own body but feeds and cares for it, just as Christ cares for the church. [30]And we are members of his body.

[31]As the Scriptures say, "A man leaves his father and mother and is joined to his wife, and the two are united into one." [32]This is a great mystery, but it is an illustration of the way Christ and the church are one. [33]So again I say, each man must love his wife as he loves himself, and the wife must respect her husband.
—Eph. 5:21–33; emphasis added

What does it look like to love your wife the same way Christ loves the church? Is there really death involved? There is death, but not literal death; the *death* in this passage refers to the death to self—the death of satisfying your earthly desires and temptations in order to truly love your wife. Her needs and wants are as important as yours; you must consider them equally.

On days when you are worn out and feeling empty, you must dig deeper. On days when she has completely rubbed you wrong and you want to be anywhere but near her, you must find forgiveness and draw strength from God, to love her even then. It means making her a priority and considering her in every decision—not because she is beautiful or because she has personality traits you enjoy, but because that is what Christ calls you to do.

Believe it or not, if you choose to love your wife in spite of her flaws and shortcomings, those things will fade over time. Those tough parts need your love the most. Through your unconditional care and love for her, those tough parts of her character will grow;

that is, she will grow in patience and become easier to love. That is good news! In *Different by Design*, John MacArthur gives a wonderful explanation of how this all works.

> That does not mean we should ignore the importance a wife's beauty, kindness, gentleness, or any other positive quality or virtue has in generating admiration from her husband. But while those qualities bring great blessing and enjoyment, they are not the bond of marriage. If every appealing characteristic and virtue of his wife were to disappear, a husband is still under obligation to love her. In fact, he is under greater obligation because her need for the healing and restorative power of his selfless love is greater. That's the kind of love Christ has for His church and is therefore the kind of love every Christian husband is to have for his wife.[10]

In most cases, a new husband has every intention of being a great husband. He plans to love his wife unconditionally and be the kind of husband she can brag about. However, all too soon, he comes to the end of his ability to love his wife on his own. His love tank becomes drained, and he feels empty. He gets tired and is vulnerable to selfishness. He might start to believe that he deserves better, or at least better than he is getting from his wife. He may think that his feelings are her fault, and there must be something he could do to fill the emptiness or fix the situation. In this tired, empty place, he is vulnerable to looking in all the wrong places to fill his lack

If our God tank is full, we will have what it takes to give again.

that, unfortunately, might cause him to lose his wife's trust and damage the relationship beyond repair.

The only way to fill our empty, tired love tank is to seek God: Spend time in worship, praise Him for what He's done for you, receive love, and ask Him for help through prayer. If our God tank is full, we will have what it takes to give again.

There was a time in our marriage when Aaron and I were focused on ourselves and demanded equal time away from the home to play with our friends. He would go away on a hunting weekend with the guys, which equaled at least a couple of nights out with the girls. I would go to a women's conference for a weekend, and that would entitle him to at least a couple of Saturdays of golf.

It got really messy with lots of resentment and animosity. Focusing on ourselves didn't work. We learned to communicate better and have conversations about our feelings. What it really came down to was loving one another more than we loved ourselves. Aaron had to switch his focus from getting his needs met to meeting my needs, and I had to do the same for him. It didn't happen overnight, but as we learned to want the best for the other first, we were able to be more fulfilled by our own time away. Again, it wasn't a quick fix, but it was a long-term fix. Loving your wife first will bring you more joy and freedom in the long run.

The journey is no longer about how *you* get to where *you* are going, but how *we* get to where *we* are going. Your success and desires should be completely intertwined. That doesn't mean you don't have individual goals and desires. It means you work as hard to support her in achieving her goals as you work toward achieving your own. It means you celebrate as boldly for her achievements as you would for your own. It means you care as much about her needs and

> *The joy of giving automatically kicks back, and you receive.*

desires as you do for your own. And in this, the great cycle of give-and-take is created. You find such joy in supporting and loving your wife that she is fulfilled and able to overflow and meet your needs. The joy of giving automatically kicks back, and you receive.

As I sit here writing this book, I am in awe of how much my husband is supporting this project. I have put off finishing the book, literally, for years and felt in the last couple of months that the Lord has clearly commanded me to push forward. As I continued to create excuses and put off obedience, my husband refused to let me stay in that place. He gave me no choice but to leave the house for at least 24 hours to work on the book. Our home is rarely quiet and, with five children, the interruptions are endless. Writing at home is almost impossible. He took a day off work, made plans for him and the kids, and insisted I find a place to stay overnight, so I could write. He even encouraged me to pay for a room somewhere which, in our tight budget, made me very uncomfortable. But I did! Sixty dollars for a beautiful room in someone's home just 30 minutes from our house.

Aaron's support exemplifies the words Paul uses to conclude the Ephesians passage, *Each man must love his wife as he loves himself.* Aaron definitely loved me to make that writing trip happen. I am sure there was no part of him that really wanted the responsibility of having five children to himself; however, his desire to love and support me outweighed his personal desires.

If Aaron had made his decision out of emotion, the writing trip never would have happened. Emotions make terrible leaders. Emotions should always follow our decisions, not make the decisions. Decisions should be made out of our conviction for what's true. In marriage, the vows you took mean you are committed to love by choice, not by what feels good or comes easily. For the husband specifically, love is the number one order God gives, and it is foundational in a healthy marriage.

Take heart that when you lay down your life for the needs for your wife, there will be blessing. God never intended for you to love without it being good for you, too. Luke says, *You should remember the words of the Lord Jesus: "It is more blessed to give than to receive"* (Acts 20:35).

Do not be harsh

> *Husbands, love your wives and never treat them harshly.*
>
> —Col. 3:19

For some husbands, aggression will be something they battle. It is never okay to treat your wife harshly; you are called to love her as Christ loved the church. Harsh words or actions do not fit the model of love in Christ's example to die for us. If anger and aggression are temptations for you, consider 1 Peter 3:7, which urges husbands to treat their wives with understanding and honor:

> *In the same way, you husbands must give honor to your wives. Treat your wife with understanding as you live together. She may be weaker than you are, but she is your equal partner in God's gift of new life. Treat her as you should so your prayers will not be hindered.*
>
> —1 Peter 3:7

To honor your wife is to respect her values even if they aren't high on your list of values. Listen to her needs and choose her way instead of yours sometime. Understanding comes into play when you try to listen even when you don't see eye to eye. In the verse above, Peter mentions the weakness of women and, in the same sentence, he describes the wife as an equal partner. Weakness or no weakness, you are not above your wife in power. In God's design, you are created as equals.

Healthy sex and the husband

> *³The husband should fulfill his wife's sexual needs, and the wife should fulfill her husband's needs. ⁴The wife gives authority over her body*

> *to her husband, and the husband gives authority*
> *over his body to his wife.*
> —1 Cor. 7:3, 4

> *Do not deprive each other of sexual relations, unless*
> *you both agree to refrain from sexual intimacy*
> *for a limited time so you can give yourselves more*
> *completely to prayer. Afterward, you should come*
> *together again so that Satan won't be able to tempt*
> *you because of your lack of self-control.*
> —1 Cor. 7:5

Society pushes the idea that sex is more important to men. In reality, sex is important to marriage. It should be no surprise that the intention for sex is for both partners to think of the other person's needs first. Sometimes meeting your wife's sexual needs will include romance. Romance is usually an important part of a woman preparing for sexual intimacy, and romance looks different to everyone; so, talk about it. In meeting your wife's sexual needs, think big picture not just in the bedroom. Pursue her and love on her hours and even days before you expect to be naked with her. In the end, her physical needs may be just as strong as yours. Just remember that her needs may begin or end outside the sexual act.

> *Society pushes the idea that sex is more important to men. In reality, sex is important to marriage.*

1 Corinthians 7:4 says that the wife has authority over her husband's body and vice versa. *Authority* is a strong word. The word in Hebrew is *exousiazō* and literally means "have authority over." So, what does it mean to allow your wife to have authority over your body? She does not have to share your body with anyone. Your body is for your wife and your wife only. In the same way, the husband is given authority over his wife's body. She gives that authority over

to him. In 1 Corinthians 7:3, we see that the intended application of this authority is to please each other.

You are given authority over your wife's body, and just as Ephesians asks you to use your leadership to put her first, Corinthians asks you to use your authority to please and serve her sexually.

To wrap up, in Colossians 3:5, Paul recognizes mankind's lack of self-control and vulnerability to temptation. If you and your wife withhold sex from one another, you are opening the door to temptation.

> *We don't ever want to give Satan even a keyhole to slither through. Keep him out! Keep sex in!*

The Bible recognizes this and instructs us not to allow temptation into our marriages. Satan will enter your marriage and begin attacking if you are not meeting one another's sexual needs. We don't ever want to give Satan even a keyhole to slither through. Keep him out! Keep sex in!

In Proverbs 5, the author uses seductive words to describe promiscuous women, warning about the consequence of giving in to their seduction, and the beauty of enjoying your wife. Talk about temptation!

> *¹My son, pay attention to my wisdom;*
> *listen carefully to my wise counsel.*
> *²Then you will show discernment,*
> *and your lips will express what you've learned.*
> *³For the lips of an immoral woman are as sweet as honey,*
> *and her mouth is smoother than oil.*
> *⁴But in the end she is as bitter as poison,*
> *as dangerous as a double-edged sword.*
> *⁵Her feet go down to death;*
> *her steps lead straight to the grave.*

⁶For she cares nothing about the path to life.
She staggers down a crooked trail and doesn't realize it.

⁷So now, my sons, listen to me.
Never stray from what I am about to say:
⁸Stay away from her!
Don't go near the door of her house!
⁹If you do, you will lose your honor
and will lose to merciless people all you have achieved.
¹⁰Strangers will consume your wealth,
and someone else will enjoy the fruit of your labor.
¹¹In the end you will groan in anguish
when disease consumes your body.
¹²You will say, "How I hated discipline!
If only I had not ignored all the warnings!
¹³Oh, why didn't I listen to my teachers?
Why didn't I pay attention to my instructors?
¹⁴I have come to the brink of utter ruin,
and now I must face public disgrace."

¹⁵Drink water from your own well—
share your love only with your wife.
¹⁶Why spill the water of your springs in the streets,
having sex with just anyone?
¹⁷You should reserve it for yourselves.
Never share it with strangers.

¹⁸Let your wife be a fountain of blessing for you.
Rejoice in the wife of your youth.
¹⁹She is a loving deer, a graceful doe.
Let her breasts satisfy you always.
May you always be captivated by her love.
²⁰Why be captivated, my son, by an immoral woman,
or fondle the breasts of a promiscuous woman?

²¹For the Lord sees clearly what a man does,
examining every path he takes.
²²An evil man is held captive by his own sins;
they are ropes that catch and hold him.
²³He will die for lack of self-control;
he will be lost because of his great foolishness.

—Prov. 5

Proverbs 5 grabs my attention every time, and I hope it does yours. Temptation is ever-present; it can come in many forms. Proverbs 5:8 gives advice for the married man tempted to stray. Don't even go near her door! In the same way, adultery doesn't begin when you go to bed with another woman. It begins when you go near "the door." In our culture, that can start with clicking on a pornographic website, staring a few extra seconds at the cleavage in front of you at work or school, or confiding in a female friend about personal issues or, God forbid, how your wife isn't meeting your every need. Every one of these acts is a small step toward a larger act. It is putting your foot on the doorstep of sharing yourself with another woman. Remember that the husband gives his wife authority over his body, so keep off all other doorsteps. Be faithful in the small things.

WIVES

What does it mean to be a wife according to God's plan? We begin by remembering that the creation story puts husband and wife on level playing ground—"from his side to be equal to him."[11] God was purposeful to make Eve out of Adam's rib, not his head or feet. Neither one is above the other or subservient to the other. Husband and wife should begin and end the journey standing next to one another as a team.

As we dive into the scripture and what it says about being a godly wife, remember this point as our foundation. As husband and wife, we stand as partners, we are on the same team. We are just given different directives to carry out our side of the partnership.

In the creation story, Adam exclaims, "At last!" He is happy to have his wife. In the preceding section for husbands, we learned that a wife is a good thing, a blessing and reward. The commentary by Jamieson, Fausset, and Brown says that the wife was created from the rib to be held dear. Let's learn how we can be that good blessing and reward.

Make sure you are a blessing

The role of the husband is to lay down his life for his wife as Christ loved the church, no matter what. Sometimes we make it very difficult for our husbands to do that. We get in the way of good things we could be receiving from our husbands—so much so that our husbands would rather be anywhere but with us. Consider these verses in Proverbs that paint a clear picture of how miserable a wife can make life for herself and her husband.

> *A worthy wife is a crown for her husband,*
> *but a disgraceful woman is like cancer in his bones.*
> —Prov. 12:4

> *It's better to live alone in the corner of an attic*
> *than **with a quarrelsome wife** in a lovely home.*
> —Prov. 21:9; emphasis added

> *It's better to live alone in the desert*
> *than **with a quarrelsome, complaining wife**.*
> —Prov. 21:19; emphasis added

Those are strong statements about the power the wife has over her husband's happiness, but the author of Proverbs doesn't just leave it at that. He gives us the remedy to the misery, so we can do something about it. The sure way to make our husbands miserable is to be quarrelsome and complaining. If a wife takes great care to speak to her husband with kindness and uses words that uplift, she will be a crown. After reading about the depths of misery in Proverbs, any woman should be interested in being her husband's crown!

A wife trusts her husband's leadership

> *The man who finds a wife finds a treasure,*
> *and he receives favor from the Lord.*
> —Prov. 18:22

> *The wife God gives you is your reward for all your*
> *earthly toil.*
> —Eccles. 9:9

Now that's what I'm talking about! That is what a wife should strive for. She should be a treasure and reward for her husband. Beyond trying not to be quarrelsome and complaining, what does that look like? How do we become treasures that our husbands can be proud of? We already established in chapter 4 that a wife is to submit to her husband out of respect for his leadership in the household. Let's look at the submission passage again and break it down a little bit.

> [21] *And further, submit to one another out of reverence for Christ.* [22]*For wives, this means submit to your husbands as to the Lord.* [23]*For a husband is the head of his wife as Christ is the head of the church. He is the Savior of his body, the church.* [24]*As the church submits to Christ, so you wives should submit to your husbands in everything.* [25]*For husbands, this means love your wives, just as Christ loved the church. He gave up his life for her* [26]*to make her holy and clean, washed by the*

*cleansing of God's word. ²⁷He did this to present her to himself as a glorious church without a spot or wrinkle or any other blemish. Instead, she will be holy and without fault. ²⁸In the same way, husbands ought to love their wives as they love their own bodies. For a man who loves his wife shows love for himself. ²⁹No one hates his own body but feeds and cares for it, just as Christ cares for the church. ³⁰And we are members of his body. ³¹As the Scriptures say, "A man leaves his father and mother and is joined to his wife, and the two are united into one." ³²This is a great mystery, but it is an illustration of the way Christ and the church are one. ³³So again I say, each man must love his wife as he loves himself, and **the wife must respect her husband**.*

—Eph. 5:21–33; emphasis added

Right off the bat, this passage says that the husband and the wife are to submit to one another out of reverence or respect for Christ. Christ is the center and the reason for this submission. Therefore, Christ is the one who defines what this means. Notice the submission involves both the husband and the wife; that makes it a two-way street. The next verse illustrates what that street looks like. The street looks a lot like the one Jesus walked to lay his life down for our needs first. A wife submits to her husband's servant leadership, and a husband lays his life down in service to his wife as Christ loved the church.

Before we get specific about what it means to be a submissive wife, we need to deal with how we feel about the word *submit*. To submit is to yield to authority. God created man to be the head of the household and woman to submit to his authority. Most people don't like the way this sounds. We like being independent; we don't want to yield to anything or anyone. Some of us may have had a bad experience with abuse and wonder if we are supposed to just submit and let that happen again. The idea of submitting may put a bad taste in your mouth for good reason—I get it! I have many friends who completely avoid this verse because of how awful it tastes.

Maybe you feel as though your husband never considers your needs. Maybe things always have to be done his way or in his timing. Maybe you don't feel heard, and by golly, you have some good ideas.

Let's pause for a minute on the word *submit*. I looked up the word *submit* in my thesaurus to find out what other words our culture uses that have a similar meaning. I laughed out loud because one of the synonyms is to "eat crow." Well, that doesn't sound any better. Some of the synonyms have negative connotations and some have positive connotations.

Positive	Negative
Abide	Cave
Acknowledge	Eat Crow
Bend	Give in
Go with the Flow	Put up with

The words on the negative list reflect our fear of submission as weakness. We typically perceive someone who submits, caves, and gives in as being mousy and always doing whatever people tell them. On the other hand, the positive list is full of helpful words. A person from this list works with, bends, and moves with the flow instead of against it. For me, the left column represents ways I want to treat my husband, and the right column represents attitudes and actions that will do neither of us any good.

Now consider the antonyms of *submit*: disobey, fight, and resist. Interestingly, these words sound a lot like the miserable wife in Proverbs.

The "negative" synonyms sound better than the antonyms, for sure. Are you with me? The good news is that God's directions are always for our good; therefore, submission should be a positive thing. We don't have to just put up with our husbands. If God intended that, he would not have called the husband to submit and serve in return. This calling to submission only works for our good if the husband says "yes" to being worthy of submission. As I said before, it's a two-way street.

So, if submission is intended for good, let's be specific about how to apply it. Ephesians 5:33 gives one example of submission by asking the wife to respect her husband. Your husband was created to need respect. He was made to protect and provide for his family. God asks you to do the very thing that will cut right to the heart of his needs and communicate love the most. But, can you do it? Can you listen to him, hear his needs, desires, and guidance? Can you acknowledge what you have heard and give weight to it? Our answer to these questions may depend on the man we are listening to, hearing, and acknowledging. His "yes" to God matters.

This is one of the most important reasons to marry a Christian. If you are putting your trust in this man as the leader of your home and you are committing to submit to his leadership, don't you want him to be consulting God on all his decisions? Don't you want him to say "yes" to the call to serve you and lay down his life for you so that it will be joyful to submit?

The husband who is committed to his vows to love you will be easy to respect and give special regard. He will stand out above all others in your eyes.

In 1 Peter 3, we are given a beautiful illustration of what it means to be a godly wife. It is not about outward beauty, but about our hearts. An unfading beauty comes from a gentle and quiet heart. How we accept our husband's leadership makes the list of inner beauty.

> *³Don't be concerned about the outward beauty of fancy hairstyles, expensive jewelry, or beautiful clothes. ⁴You should clothe yourselves instead with the beauty that comes from within, the unfading*

> *beauty of a gentle and quiet spirit, which is so*
> *precious to God. ⁵This is how the holy women of old*
> *made themselves beautiful. They trusted God and*
> *accepted the authority of their husbands.*
>
> —1 Pet. 3:3–5

Did you also notice from 1 Peter that accepting your husband's authority takes trust in God? If God has your back, you can let go of whether your husband is making the right decision. You will find peace—peace in letting go of control, assuming your husband is capable, and knowing that God is. The result will be peace in your home and marriage and peace in your heart. When you commit to praying for your husband and then agree with decisions that he makes, you can relax a little bit. It's not bad to let someone else make the decisions every now and then, right?

But let's not downplay the call of the wife. This isn't easy. This isn't a submission for when we feel like it, or when we want to, or when our husband is trustworthy. The submission you are to give your husband is directly compared to the submission we give to Christ. It is complete trust and respect in everything and in all decisions. Your flesh will not like this kind of surrender. You will fight it. This level of surrender is definitely possible, but only if you walk into marriage with these goals in mind. Give yourself mercy and strive to do better each day. Don't be too concerned with your physical beauty. Take care of yourself, be healthy, but spend the most time working on your inward beauty. Be gentle with a quiet heart instead of quarrelsome and complaining. Partner with and encourage your husband: *Wives, submit to your husbands, as is fitting for those who belong to the Lord (Col. 3:18).*

She manages the home

Proverbs 31:10–31 illustrate a beautiful picture of a woman managing the home. While tending to her inner beauty and character in her relationship with her husband, she still has great responsibility in making sure the household is run smoothly. This wife of noble character in Proverbs 31 seems too good to be true, but hey, let's dream for a moment about what's possible.

A Wife of Noble Character
¹⁰Who can find a virtuous and capable wife?
She is more precious than rubies.
¹¹Her husband can trust her,
and she will greatly enrich his life.
¹²She brings him good, not harm,
all the days of her life.

¹³She finds wool and flax
and busily spins it.
¹⁴She is like a merchant's ship,
bringing her food from afar.
¹⁵She gets up before dawn to prepare breakfast for her household
and plan the day's work for her servant girls.

¹⁶She goes to inspect a field and buys it;
with her earnings she plants a vineyard.
¹⁷She is energetic and strong,
a hard worker.
¹⁸She makes sure her dealings are profitable;
her lamp burns late into the night.

¹⁹Her hands are busy spinning thread,
her fingers twisting fiber.
²⁰She extends a helping hand to the poor
and opens her arms to the needy.
²¹She has no fear of winter for her household,
for everyone has warm clothes.

²²She makes her own bedspreads.
She dresses in fine linen and purple gowns.

²³Her husband is well known at the city gates,
where he sits with the other civic leaders.
²⁴She makes belted linen garments
and sashes to sell to the merchants.

²⁵She is clothed with strength and dignity,
and she laughs without fear of the future.
²⁶When she speaks, her words are wise,
and she gives instructions with kindness.
²⁷She carefully watches everything in her household
and suffers nothing from laziness.

²⁸Her children stand and bless her.
Her husband praises her:
²⁹"There are many virtuous and capable women in the world,
but you surpass them all!"

³⁰Charm is deceptive, and beauty does not last;
but a woman who fears the Lord will be greatly praised.
³¹Reward her for all she has done.
Let her deeds publicly declare her praise.

—Prov. 31:10–31

Wouldn't you like to be as precious as a ruby, clothed in strength and dignity, blessed and praised by your family? To get there, you start with today. Do the best you can, one day at a time, as God leads you.

Compare your progress only with your own goals. Keep a journal and read it and be encouraged by how your improving. The worst thing you can do is compare yourself with another wife or single woman. We all put our best foot forward and our best pictures on Facebook. If you compare yourself to that, you will never be good enough or satisfied with your efforts. Remember, that picture of a perfectly prepared dinner on a pristinely set table waiting for her handsome husband may, in reality, be the first time she has cooked anything all month. Instead of comparing yourself to the Pinterest wife next door, focus on you. Evaluate your growth by asking yourself these questions:

1. Do I know God more every day?
2. Am I leaning on and trusting my husband more every day?
3. Does my family/husband feel cared for in my work around the home?

Healthy sex and the wife

> [3] *The husband should fulfill his wife's sexual needs, and the wife should fulfill her husband's needs.* [4] *The wife gives authority over her body to her husband, and the husband gives authority over his body to his wife.* [5] *Do not deprive each other of sexual relations, unless you both agree to refrain from sexual intimacy for a limited time so you can give yourselves more completely to prayer. Afterward, you should come together again so that Satan won't be able to tempt you because of your lack of self-control.*
>
> —1 Cor. 7:3–5

These are the same scriptures we studied in the section for the husband because everything in these verses creates impartiality, both from the giving side and the receiving side. Both the husband and the wife are to please, fulfill, and not deprive. Neither one's needs are superior to the other.

Society often pushes the idea that once a couple gets married, the woman never wants to have sex. Even though there are lots of couples that prove this wrong, there is a reason men worry that this may be true. The truth is, sometimes meeting your husband's needs will be the last thing you are in the mood for, but scripture encourages you to make the choice out of love for your husband.

Choosing to serve your husband in this way will communicate love, respect, and acceptance.

Maybe you feel like this is asking too much. After all, you've worked hard all day and you should be able to sleep if you need to instead of serving yet again. Physical intimacy takes energy. You are called to submit to your husband because of your love for him. The husband is given authority over his wife. Remember the husband is called to lay his needs aside to serve you, which brings with it a great deal of personal cost and responsibility. He has a very important part of the contract to uphold. You uphold your end, so that he can more completely uphold his. Sex can be fun and fulfilling in marriage. Don't withhold that from your husband or yourself. Some nights you may be tired or not in the mood, but push through on a regular basis. What starts out as personal sacrifice and losing a little sleep will end up satisfying and sometimes even fun. In the end, the benefits of a healthy sex life are worth losing a little extra sleep.

In the section for husbands, we covered the real and present danger of giving Satan any room to wiggle into your marriage; withholding sex is absolutely a way to do this.

> *[18]Let your wife be a fountain of blessing for you.*
> *Rejoice in the wife of your youth.*
> *[19]She is a loving deer, a graceful doe.*
> *Let her breasts satisfy you always.*
> *May you always be captivated by her love.*
>
> —Prov. 5:18–19

Being mindful to please your husband will also keep sexual temptation in check. Colossians 3:5 takes that point deeper and asserts that sex will help with self-control. The Bible speaks very directly to men about temptation. But wives, don't skip over this warning for you too. Temptation comes in all forms, and women are not exempt. Set boundaries to guard yourself from things you know will tempt you—whether it's pornography, flirting, a handsome man you like to look at, or a male friend you are tempted to confide in for emotional support. Protect yourself. Never underestimate the power of sexual intimacy in marriage to draw you together in your service to each other and to keep your sexual needs focused inside the marriage. By being the wife God instructs you to be, you will create an environment that leads your husband to be the man God is calling him to be.

Chapter 6

Continue Pursuing Your Long-Term Goals

*G*oals are very important both while you are single and after you are married. As a single, you can focus all your energy on your personal goals and make great strides in reaching them. Make sure that you aren't wasting time by being too focused on finding your spouse or getting to the altar when you could be developing YOU. Think about all the things you can accomplish while you are waiting. As a single, you have so much more time and freedom to focus on yourself than you will ever have again. Discover your greatest passions and strongest talents. Seek what God has in store for you and prepare yourself so you are ready when opportunity comes knocking on your door.

When you tie the knot, you will be committing to divide your time between your goals and desires and your spouse's goals and desires. Of course, you will draw strength from having a partner supporting and encouraging you. The struggle is that your time and energy will be more divided.

In this chapter, we will look at five areas in which we can continue to grow throughout life. The healthier each of these areas is, the healthier your single life and your marriage will be. The list of focus areas will look a little different for everyone, but we can all grow in these areas:

> Finances
> Career
> Relationships
> Gifts and Talents
> Faith

There is nothing like focusing on long-term goals and personal growth to keep you living in the present.

Finances

In this section, I write primarily to singles, but all the ideas and suggestions can apply to married couples as well. There is always room to have more personal freedom when it comes to our finances. Debt can weigh us down. Maybe you made a choice to borrow money for education and now are loaded down with school loans. Or maybe, in an effort to be a grown up, you spent money buying and furnishing your first place. Let's not forget the needful purchases such as cars to get to and from work. And for some, the 1 Corinthians 6:12 passage we studied regarding sexual temptation also applies here. Perhaps you have become a slave to your spending whims, and shopping and collecting more and more things has become an addiction. Be honest with yourself. Is it shoes, tools, or a kicked-up truck where you are tempted to overspend? Or maybe you're an emotional shopper who spends to make yourself feel better in the moment. Debt, for whatever reason, straps you down. Credit gives you the allusion of freedom, but in the end, it weighs you down.

Maybe debt is not the issue. For you, it might be learning the discipline of saving money and having financial goals. Freedom comes from being debt-free, and there is an even greater level of freedom when you have savings set aside for those unexpected expenditures such as car break-downs, medical emergencies, or whatever else might come up. Perhaps you will be able to take a trip with friends or family because you have money already saved up. That's definitely something I would prefer to spend my savings on. Savings bring financial freedom.

Now is the time to be intentional with your spending and saving. Create a plan for your financial freedom. Make a budget that is realistic for your income and expenses. There are lots of places to get help with this. Talk with friends and family to get recommendations for a good financial advisor or a local class. I recommend any Dave Ramsey books or classes; he has been our favorite source of information for keeping on track financially. His books and training walk you step by step to financial freedom. Although the journey may be uncomfortable up front, financial freedom will be worth the effort.

Set a goal for financial freedom as a gift to you and your future (or current) spouse. Who wants to marry into someone else's financial mess? Starting a marriage financially upright is a lot more fun than starting it upside down. Pray that your future spouse is preparing the same financial gift for you.

If you are married, you may already know that money is the number one topic of arguments in marriages. The good news is you don't have to accept that in your relationship. Set goals together, offer lots of grace, and talk regularly about your budget. You are a team when it comes to finances. Don't try to be right; focus on a joint win when it comes to money!

Career

If you are single, chances are you are in school preparing for a future career or have already begun a career. Make the most of this time while you are only responsible for yourself. You may never have another time in your life when you only have to worry about yourself. Your busy schedule, lack of sleep, and missed meals don't affect anyone except you. Actively move forward in your career. Of course, you can still make awesome career advancements after you are married and have the support of a spouse, but the stronger base you have, the better. And the pace at which you move forward could slow down when you begin to divide your time, consider someone else's schedule, or start a family.

For me, it wasn't about the career. Although I received a master's degree in an area I am passionate about, my ultimate goal was always to be a full-time mom. My career in Early Childhood Special Education was short lived, but I made the most of it while I could. My pre-marriage and pre-baby time was when I could enjoy my career and use that education. I don't know that I will ever step back into that world, but I'm thankful for the time I had before I was married and had children.

Once you have a family, career should always take a back seat to that family or spouse. That doesn't mean you neglect your work responsibilities; it just means to always double check that your family is your priority. In *Choosing to Cheat*, Andy Stanley says you must choose to cheat work, or your family will be cheated.[12]

Friendships

Friendships come and go. Some are for a season, and some are lifelong. Some are life-giving, and others are draining and toxic. I am sure you know what I mean. We should always be evaluating the health of our friendships, weeding out the unhealthy ones, and cutting strings where needed, so we have our relationships in order. A friend who drains you, leads you to temptation, or influences you in a negative way will not be a healthy third party in your marriage.

Sometimes a friendship might be healthy, but there may be baggage between that friend and you. For example, you might be harboring anger, or forgiveness may be needed. Maybe you need to ask for forgiveness, or maybe you need to give it—either way do what you can to mend that relationship. Don't forget to evaluate family relationships as well. The relationship that needs attention may be someone as close as your parents or siblings. Whatever you can do to mend relationships with family will be good for you and much appreciated by your spouse.

Gifts and Talents

What gifts and talents has God planted in you? Do you already have a hobby that you are passionate about? Is there a talent you are still developing but feel drawn to? Maybe there is a skill that you would love to develop but haven't made time for yet. There is no better time than when you are single. Once you are married, you might look back on your time as a single person and regret not taking advantage of the time to be focused on these things. Still, it is good not to forget or give up on these kinds of desires once you are married.

My husband has personal experience with this. In high school, he was state-ranked in pole vaulting. He excelled his junior year and breezed through district competitions; he vaulted right through regionals and landed a spot to compete at state. I was the proud girlfriend cheering him on from the sidelines with his mother sitting on my left and my mother sitting on my right.

His senior year, I could hardly wait to sit in those bleachers again to cheer him on. That opportunity never came. He was too focused on the future instead of the present. "Senioritis" had set in, and he wanted to be finished with high school more than anything. He lackadaisically trained for his upcoming senior track season, only doing what he had to do to get by, checking it off his to-do list you might say. We couldn't see it then, but looking back, he was too focused on me and college and not focused on the opportunities right in front of him. His track season came and went with little excitement. He didn't even make it to district competitions, and in the moment, that was okay with him because he had his eyes on the next phase of life, college. Now, he looks back and would tell you that it was time wasted. He sees all the potential there was for growth, success, and celebrations. He missed out because he was already focused on the next big thing. If he could have focused his energy on the present, he might have made it to state again and created memories and achievements to celebrate forever. He will never get those opportunities back. Trying to skip forward to college didn't get him to the dorm any sooner.

What about you? Develop your skills, take a class, and run that marathon. God may have big plans for the desires he has planted in you.

Faith

Since faith has been the focus of our conversations thus far, I will be a huge cheerleader for this topic. Start here! End here! Continue here! Spend time here! I hope that, after reading this book, you will commit to marrying someone who is journeying down a similar path of faith as you. Regardless of your spouse's faith, yours should be as solid as possible. Your spiritual maturity will affect your ability to ease into the transition of marriage. The more acquainted you are with who you are in Christ, the more prepared you will be for marriage. The more you are filled and fulfilled by Jesus, the healthier your marriage will be. The more frequently you allow the Spirit to guide you, the better wife or husband you will be.

Never stop leaning into the truth of your identity in Christ. You are a child of God, you are fearfully and wonderfully made, you can do all things through Christ, and you are worth dying for. Believing these things changes how you walk through this world. Soak this truth in. You are made to love and be loved. God has purposed you for something very specific. He orders your steps. The more

> *Never stop leaning into the truth of your identity in Christ: You are a child of God, you are fearfully and wonderfully made, you can do all things through Christ, and you are worth dying for.*

you are able to live with confidence in these truths, the more you will be able to join with your spouse and strengthen one another.

Let Go of the Fantasy

I believe one of the biggest disappointments in marriage is that we expect our newfound love to "complete us" and fill the empty places in our hearts. In our minds, marriage is a fantasy land of having our needs met, making life easier, and having loneliness swept away.

By now, you have read enough to know that this fantasy isn't reality. You've made the paradigm shift to know that marriage isn't about getting your needs met but about focusing on your spouse's needs. Keep yourself in check and reflect on where this fantasy may still exist in your heart. We all have longings for a better life that only Jesus can offer. Reflect on ways you want a spouse to make your life better. Are you hoping for someone who can read your mind and know what to say and when to say it, give you sex as often as you want it, romance you forever and always, and recognize how hard you work? Maybe they'll even have the house picked up, the laundry done, and dinner ready when you get home in the evening.

The reality is that marriage is a relationship in which you are to submit and serve. Jesus set the bar high. If you are single, this is a good time to practice letting go of the fantasy of being served in marriage. Practice serving and getting your needs met by Jesus now. Join a Bible study, go on a mission trip, or build a house with Habitat for Humanity. Allow Jesus to be enough and to be your closest confidant. Learn about spiritual intimacy through prayer. Learn about the Holy Spirit and practice recognizing how to discern his nudges and guidance. If you are married, never stop seeking these things and growing in these areas. All these things can mend, grow, and strengthen your marriage.

There is no better path than the one God will lead you down. Take time to recognize how God speaks to you in that still, small voice when life is quiet. After you are married, there will be another voice giving input and guidance. The more you recognize God's voice now, the clearer it will be later when there is another louder, tangible voice right next to you. Just think, that same voice of the Holy Spirit may one day confirm when you have met your prospective spouse and should say "yes." What a gift!

To those still looking forward to marriage:

> *When you look back on this time of waiting, you'll want to congratulate yourself for the time well spent. You'll want to say this was one of the best times of your life. Is there a bodacious dream you've always been scared to step into? DO IT! Anything from becoming a fitness competitor to working at Starbucks to learning to speak Chinese. DO IT! Have an adventure and accomplish something totally out of your comfort zone but completely fulfilling. You never know, that adventure just might lead you to the love of your life.*

Chapter 7

The Final Stretch

¹Finally, then, brothers, we ask and urge you in the Lord Jesus, that as you received from us how you ought to walk and to please God, just as you are doing, that you do so more and more. ²For you know what instructions we gave you through the Lord Jesus. ³For this is the will of God, your sanctification: that you abstain from sexual immorality; ⁴that each one of you know how to control his own body in holiness and honor, ⁵not in the passion of lust like the Gentiles who do not know God; ⁶that no one transgress and wrong his brother in this matter, because the Lord is an avenger in all these things, as we told you beforehand and solemnly warned you. ⁷For God has not called us for impurity, but in holiness. ⁸Therefore whoever disregards this, disregards not man but God, who gives his Holy Spirit to you.

—1 Thess. 4:1–8 ESV

A Life Pleasing to God

Now the reality of your life is in front of you. It's up to you to take in all this information about marriage and apply it. From the earlier chapters, you should have a clearer picture of marriage: who it was created by, what it was created for, and what is expected of you.

Whether you are ready to find a spouse or marriage is far off, you should have a better understanding of how to prepare for and walk down the aisle. You have a new framework for waiting and growing in marriage.

In the first chapter, we talked about the progression of life and two ways to walk down the aisle. You can marry out of desperation and settle for something that might not last, or you can trust God, make the most of your time, and wait for someone who understands commitment and living out what God intended for marriage.

A Tale of Two Wedding Days

I have written an illustration of these two ways to enter into marriage. As you read the scenarios that follow, pay attention to which one represents the hope you have for your wedding day.

Wedding Scenario #1

The bride and groom are both excited about their big day. They have been planning for almost a year. The bride feels she has been waiting her whole life for this day, and finally all her plans are coming together. Over the past year, the groom has been along for the ride of planning and, to be honest, is ready to move beyond choosing flowers and cake.

The bride looks in the mirror and feels like she is dreaming. She is excited to see herself dressed in white with perfect hair and make-up and wearing jewelry chosen especially for this day; everyone is ready to help at her beck and call. It is almost too good to be true.

For a moment, she thinks about the last fight she and her groom had. *We still haven't agreed on how to set up our finances as a married couple. He wants one checking account, but I want my own money that he can't question me about. He doesn't need to know every time I spend money. But we decided to deal with that later.* But then she stops her thoughts. *Enough of that, this is my big day, I need to enjoy every minute of MY day!*

Down the hall, the groom is playing cards with his groomsmen to pass the time. They are laughing, throwing jokes back and forth, making the most of the groom's last moments of being single. One of his groomsmen elbows him and says, "Hey man, this is it! One woman for the rest of your life," adding a big grin to really drive home his remark. Everyone laughs, including the groom, but his mind begins to wander, *Man, this IS it! What will it be like to be with the same woman for the rest of my life? We have a lot of fun together. We love hanging out with friends, running together, and spending the weekends out on the water. We have a great sex life too. Sure, we fight about money, but we can work that out later, right? Man, what if sex gets boring? What if she becomes a nagging and complaining wife? What we have is good for now. If it doesn't last forever, it won't be the first time a marriage breaks up.*

Wedding Scenario #2

Everyone has begun gathering at the downtown church for their special day. The bride and groom feel like they have waited forever. Today, it will finally be official, the beginning of their lives as husband and wife. They haven't seen each other since the rehearsal dinner ended last night, and yet it seems like forever. They have prayer together that God would join them on this day and always be part of their marriage. They both believe that only with God can their marriage be lifelong and fulfilling for both of them.

The bride is in the parlor with her bridesmaids and a few family members. Her dress is all she ever dreamed of. Her bouquet just arrived; it is so beautiful that it took her breath away. She can't stop smiling. Still, her thoughts keep drifting to when they return from their honeymoon and begin their life journey together. *When will we buy our first home? When will we start our family? What will our first big disagreement be about as husband and wife?* As she peers out the window, she daydreams. *What will it be like when we celebrate grandchildren together? Will we ever get to check off all the destinations on our list of places we want to travel together? What will our greatest challenges be?* The one thing she doesn't question is how they will navigate through all of that. They have already agreed that God will constantly be part of their marriage. She believes with all her heart that God can bring them through anything.

Downstairs, the groom is sitting with his groomsmen, sharing old stories. They are laughing and poking fun about their good old college days. The groom's nerves continue to remind him the ceremony is drawing near. As much as he is ready to marry his bride, he has dreaded the actual ceremony. All eyes will be on them, and he is not one to enjoy the spotlight. Nonetheless, he wouldn't change any of it for the world. He can hardly wait for the minister to announce them as husband and wife. He has loved her for so long, and now it will be official. They will be joined in the Holy Sacrament of marriage. As his groomsmen continue telling stories of wild nights and girlfriends of the past, his thoughts wander to his new life. *What will it be like to be a husband? It will be nice to come home to her every day. What if my career doesn't go as I imagined? I am responsible for providing for our family now. What if the sex isn't as exciting as I imagined? Will I be able to go out with the guys without a guilt trip when I get home?* Then he snaps back to his commitment to trust in God, *Stop! Everything will be fine. We have asked God to be the center of our marriage. When times are tough, we won't be alone. We will fight our way through it as a team. We've got this.*

And at that thought, the pastor walks in to let them know it is time for the ceremony. The cousins have begun lighting the candles. The groom thinks he might actually throw up because his nerves just flipped his stomach—only because of the eyes that will be on him and his bride. His bride! Yes, his bride. This is their special day to begin their lifelong partnership, until death do them part.

Which Path Will You Choose?

There is a clear difference between the two couples. One is focused on the wedding day but has thought almost nothing about the marriage. They are happy in the moment, but have no assurance it will last. The second couple is focused on their marriage and commitment to make it work. They have asked God to be the center of their marriage and to help them be successful.

What about you? No matter which path you have chosen in the past or what path your parents have modeled for you, a new journey can begin today. No matter your age or history, your future can involve living life with purpose to prepare for and create a successful marriage:

- Evaluate the relationship you are in. Don't waste time starting a journey with someone who is not ready to commit to marriage the way God intended.

- Create a character "must-have" list for the person you want to marry. What are the qualities you want? What are the deal-breakers? Make a decision now and stick to your must-have list, so that you will be less tempted by the wrong person later.

- Prioritize your growth. Work on your relationship with God, get your finances in order, create healthy friendships, and begin healing from any previous sexual brokenness or addictions.

- Make a promise today to yourself and your future spouse that your marriage is worth waiting for. Promise not to add any baggage that can keep you from having a fulfilling marriage. Believe that you are worth it.

- Surround yourself with friends, family, and a mentor who will lift you up and encourage you. This can literally make or break you.

- Memorize a few verses to draw strength from. Some days will be easier than others, but God is **always** right there waiting to love you and give you strength. Call out to Him in times of sadness or weakness. Here are a few of my favorite verses.

> *[35]So do not throw away this confident trust in the Lord. Remember the great reward it brings you! [36]Patient endurance is what you need now, so that you will continue to do God's will. Then you will receive all that he has promised.*
>
> —Heb. 10:35–36

> *The temptations in your life are no different from what others experience. And God is faithful. He will not allow the temptation to be more than you can stand. When you are tempted, he will show you a way out so that you can endure.*
>
> —1 Cor. 10:13

> *The Lord gives his people strength.*
> *The Lord blesses them with peace.*
>
> —Ps. 29:11

Personal Notes from the Author

*B*efore I sat down to write this book, these brief notes of encouragement came to me. I have included them on the following pages because I want you to know that you are worth the wait.

My prayer is that you will be empowered and encouraged as you anticipate your future spouse or begin making your knot worth fighting for with great hope and anticipation.

Ladies,

Be secure in who you are in Christ. Know who He has made you to be. You are beautiful, strong, courageous, loving, and can do all things through Christ because He is your Father. If you will be patient and trust your Father's plan for you, He will guide you to your prince charming. That man will not be perfect, and there will be times when your prince charming drives you crazy. Most likely he will not ride in on a white horse or save the day. He may not look anything like you imagined. It's likely that he may not kiss your hand every day, whisper sweet nothings in your ear, or even remember to put the toilet seat down! However, I can promise you that God is good, and He sees you and wants to give you more husband than you ever dreamed you could have. The husband God intended for you is worth the wait. You are worth the wait!

Gentlemen,

God has chosen a special woman for you. Prepare for her by setting yourself up for success. You will be her provider, and God has equipped you for your very own purpose on this earth. There will be many distractions that come in all forms, but keep your eye on the one who modeled servant leadership. Stand firm in waiting for someone who shares the same goals of a marriage centered on Christ, and your beautiful, loving wife will respect you for who you are, just as God made you.

God has chosen her just for you, to make you stronger and bring out the best in you. Trust in God's timing and His provision. She may not always communicate well, and sometimes will speak out of frustration and anger. Some days, you will want to give up on ever understanding how her mind works or what she really wants from you. But you can trust that deep down, she will respect, encourage, and support you. She will be worth the wait. You are worth the wait!

Appendix

Resources for Further Study

You may find the following resources helpful for further study about living as a godly single or married person:

- *Captivating: Unveiling the Mystery of a Woman's Soul*, John and Stasi Eldredge
- *Wild at Heart*, John Eldredge
- *Love and Respect*, Dr. Emerson Eggerichs
- *The 5 Love Languages*, Gary Chapman
- www.marriagetoday.com

Notes

1. Chris Hodges, "Right Beginnings," Week 1 video lecture (Parenting on Purpose, Fall, 2016).

2. Mark Driscoll, "What Are You Afraid Of?" (Presentation at Annual Catalyst Conference, Atlanta, GA, October 5–7, 2011).

3. Sarah Young, *Jesus Calling* (Nashville: Thomas Nelson, 2011), 89.

4. Beth Moore, *Entrusted* (Nashville: LifeWay Press, 2016), 76.

5. Jimmy Evans, Presentation (Lifelong Love Affair Marriage Seminar, Simulcast at Highbridge Church, Benbrook, TX, February 8–9, 2013).

6. Evans, Lifelong Love Affair Marriage Seminar.

7. "Porn Addiction Infographic," Guy Stuff, accessed September 20, 2017, https://www.guystuffcounseling.com/porn-addiction-infographic.

8. Evans, Lifelong Love Affair Marriage Seminar.

9. Robert Jamieson, Andrew Robert Fausset, and David Brown, *Commentary Critical and Explanatory on the Whole Bible* (Oak Harbor, WA: Logos Research Systems, Inc., 1997).

10. John MacArthur, Jr., *Different by Design* (Wheaton, IL: Victor Books, 1996), 71.

11. Jamieson, Fausset, and Brown.

12. Andy Stanley, *Choosing to Cheat: Who Wins When Family and Work Collide* (Colorado Springs: Multnomah Books, 2003).